Tutor
Your Child
to
Reading Success

Angela Norton Tyler

D1567196

Natomas Tutoring

2121 Natomas Crossing Drive
Suite 200-159
Sacramento, CA 95834
(916) 806-9663
www.NatomasTutoring.com

Natomas Tutoring's books, booklets and audiocassettes may be purchased for fund-raising, educational, business or sales promotional use. For more information, please see the order form at the back of this book and/ or contact Orders@NatomasTutoring.com.

The information in this book is distributed on an "as is" basis, without warranty. While every precaution has been taken in preparation of this book, and all information is deemed to be correct, neither the author nor the publisher is liable for any loss or damage caused or alleged to be caused directly or indirectly by instructions contained in this book or by other books and websites listed.

This publication is designed to provide accurate and authoritative information in regard to the subject matter covered. It is sold with the understanding that the publisher is not engaged in rendering professional tutoring or diagnostic services. If professional advice or other expert assistance is required, the services of a competent professional person should be sought.

ISBN #0-9769557-0-9

Dedication

This book is dedicated to my mother,
Eloise Norton.

Thank you for your never-wavering belief in my ability as writer.

*****

This book is also dedicated to my father,
John H. Norton, III.

Thank you for telling me on my first day of kindergarten to
sit in the front of the room and ask a lot of questions.

*****

I would like to take this opportunity to REALLY thank my sister, Meredith Norton, for not only believing that I would finish this book, but using her humor, creativity, expertise and sheer determination to make it happen. You have always been my sister, but now you are my friend and colleague. I am sorry for all of the times I wouldn't let you come into my room.

To my brother-in-law, Thibault Jousse, thank you for working so very hard on making this book look so very good!

To my husband, Kevin Tyler, thank you for taking care of the business side of the equation and letting me do my thing. It is not always easy, but I hope you think it's worth it!

And, hugs and kisses to my children, Kendall and John Calvin. You are the best teachers a mom could ever hope to have!

Acknowledgments

I have had the opportunity to work with some incredible teachers and administrators. Jon Hassell, you were a "dream principal", and I was one unbelievably lucky new teacher. Thank you for giving me my first opportunity to make a contribution. Desira Rugley, hundreds of children are out there reading because of your dedication and determination. Oh, the phonics, the phonics! Milly Schrader, if every principal were like you, schools would be full of inspired teachers and excited students. Your loving professionalism brings out the best in all.

A Plea to Parents

From the moment your children entered this world, they have needed you in a myriad of ways. Among other things, you have fed them, clothed them, and kept them out of harm's way. Now, they need something else from you. Your children need you to fully and truly believe that they can become good, strong, masterful readers *and* that you can help them do it. Your son needs you to believe that one day he will read as well as the other kids in his class. Your daughter needs you to believe that soon she will be able to read the same books that all the other kids are reading. *Do you truly believe that you can tutor your child to reading success?* Children can sense when adults are unsure, so please be confident! Knowing that you are confident in them will help them find confidence in themselves.

I have always known that parents have the *ability* to help their children read, but until a few years ago, I believed they lacked the *confidence* to try. Two changes have occurred in the last few years that prove that not only do parents want to teach their children to read, they are doing it like never before. Home schooling and the Internet are changing the face of education.

When I first began teaching, the home school movement hadn't yet become part of mainstream America. Of course, there have always been people teaching their children at home, but I thought of them as "on the fringe," literally and figuratively. I dismissed home school families figuring that they either lived in the middle of nowhere (like on an ice floe in the Arctic), were strange social extremists-or both. It never occurred to me that ordinary parents would choose to teach their children at home. But now I know that all sorts of parents are choosing to do just that. In fact, I have become a home school consultant!

The United States Department of Education reported that 1.1 million children were home schooled in 2003 (July 2004). Some groups claim that this number is even greater; all agree that the home school movement continues to grow each year. This book is not a treatise on the pros and cons of home schooling. The fact that so many parents have chosen to become their children's primary educators tells me that they have confidence in their abilities. After all, you wouldn't choose to home school your child if you believed you were incompetent! Because of the prevalence of home schooling, many parents that do not home school have come to accept the idea that parents can also be educators.

When I first began teaching, only 18% of households had Internet access;

it is now estimated that three out of five families log on at home. Nearly any information one needs or wants can be brought into one's home- and this includes the esoteric field of reading theory and practice. This unprecedented ease of access to information has given all of us, including parents and would-be teachers, the assurance that one doesn't have to be an expert in a particular field to know what's going on. The information is out there, we can find it, and we will use it!

I support anything that helps children become good, strong, excited readers, and I have worked in the past to make that a reality. Where I once focused my efforts on teachers and students in classroom settings, I now know that parents have the confidence to play a bigger role in their children's education. This book is my attempt to give parents the tools and skills they need to help their children become excellent readers. Tutor Your Child to Reading Success is for you, parents! Share your confidence and enthusiasm with your child, and watch them read!

TABLE OF CONTENTS

PART ONE

FIRST THINGS FIRST

CHAPTER 1

DOES MY CHILD NEED TUTORING?

We have never met, yet I would like to make a confession. Throughout my entire teaching career, I have felt like an impostor. I taught classes, attended staff meetings and trainings, spent personal money on classroom supplies, and the whole time I felt more like a parent than an educator, more *Mom* than *Mrs. Tyler*. Please don't misunderstand, I took my career as a teacher very seriously. I had high expectations for myself and my students, and one would be hard-pressed to find a former student or colleague of mine to say otherwise. What I am trying to express is that when I taught, I *approached* it as a parent who happened to be a teacher. When I stood in front of my class explaining a difficult concept, worked one-on-one with a struggling student, or planned next week's lesson, I did it with the thought, "If this were my child's teacher, what would I want her to do?" This feeling of being a parent first and a teacher second has shaped my career in education and produced this book, <u>Tutoring Your Child to Reading Success</u>.

Many teachers have been surprised or annoyed by the way I interact with parents. Basically, I am honest and direct regarding their child's academics and behavior. I don't want teachers holding anything back from me about my own children, so I won't do it to other parents. I have found that most parents appreciate my candor and honesty. They would rather be told that their daughter is flunking math because she doesn't know her multiplication tables instead of, "Oh, Madison is a little behind, but I am sure she will catch up soon!" Sugarcoating information today only hurts children later. I won't do it.

Some teachers did not appreciate it when I told them to stop blinding and bombarding parents with interesting, but unnecessary information. For example, before parent-teacher conferences, teachers would scurry around making a million copies of rubrics and studies and reading lists and anything else they could get their hands on to give to parents. Not only was all of this work a waste of time, paper and copy machine toner, my contention was that parents didn't want another packet of information. Teachers were horrified!

Didn't I think that parents cared about their children? Yes, I think that parents care about their children! Did I think that parents wanted pages and pages of educational research? No. Most parents I know are strapped for time and they don't want another packet to decipher. A six page study on homework may be interesting to educators, but parents want to know this teacher's homework expectations this year. Why not give parents the information they want and need as succinctly as possible? This belief did not make me popular with Packet Crazy Teachers.

As a parent myself, I know that most parents want to know two things:

How is my child doing in school?

and

What can I do at home to help?

That's it. That is what parents want to know. As a teacher, I was usually able to answer the first question quite easily. I had grades, papers, homework and hours and hours of classroom observation. I knew a student's strengths and weaknesses, and could easily share that information with a parent. It was the second question that I found so difficult to answer, especially when it came to reading.

Most teachers would like nothing better than for parents to take an active role in their children's education, and I was no different. I had suggestions for parents (read with them *every* night, use flash cards, get a tutor), but I never felt that I was able to give parents what they *really* needed- a simple, easy-to-follow reading program designed especially for them. The books or programs I did manage to find were either written for those studying for their teaching credential (too detailed, too much theory), teachers with full classrooms (lessons not easily applicable), or didn't address all three components of reading, which we will discuss in ***Chapter 2 How Children Learn to Read.***

When I left the classroom and began to tutor privately, I created my own tutoring program which included simple and easy homework lessons for parents to do with their children. The homework reinforced what my students had learned with me and only took a few minutes each day. Students received intensive, individual instruction during private tutoring sessions plus reinforcement at home. It should have come as no surprise, yet I was amazed by my students' progress. They were learning new words, reading faster and more accurately, and most importantly, they *understood* what they had read. I patted myself on the back for being such a great tutor, but, finally, I had to admit something to myself. Most of what I did could be done by any competent and patient adult. My students didn't need me, or any other "outside" tutor. With a little direction and encouragement, I knew that their own parents were perfectly capable of doing my job themselves.

So, I wrote this book and put myself out of a tutoring job!

Please notice, I said tutoring job, not *teaching* job. <u>Tutor Your Child to Reading Success</u> is not a comprehensive reading program meant to be your first and only approach to teaching reading. It is a reading bridge, taking children from where they are, to where they should be. This book is my answer to the question "What can I do at home to help?" It shows parents how to determine whether or not their child is reading at grade level and, if not, what to do to change the situation. Once parents figure out what their child needs to learn, they are shown how to teach it.

Before we dive into this book and discuss what we can do at home to help, let's consider how your child is doing in school. How can you be sure that your child even needs tutoring?

There are different ways to determine whether or not your child needs tutoring. The first and most important clue is your intuition. I cannot count the times that a parent has said, "I'm not sure exactly how far behind he is, but I know something isn't right. I know he needs help." Most parents don't need a reading specialist to tell them that their child isn't reading at grade-level. Parents are attuned to their children's academic struggles, even if sometimes they are unable to pinpoint them exactly. Trust your gut instinct as you have countless other times while raising your children.

Sadly, I have also had parents tell me that they knew something was wrong years before, but didn't do anything about it. "The teacher didn't make a big deal about it, and he was promoted to the next grade, so I just thought I'd wait and *see*." Hearing that breaks my heart. If you *ever* have a feeling that your child isn't reading as well as she should be, do something (like use this book)! Don't second guess yourself, and please don't feel that you must wait for the teacher to tell you that your child needs reading help.

That's not to say that you should not talk to your child's teacher! If the teacher indicates during a parent-teacher conference, on a report card, note, email or phone call that your child is not reading at grade level, please listen and respond! And by all means, if you have concerns, don't wait until conference time to approach your child's teacher. Ask, "Do you feel that Jordan is reading at grade level?" We are talking about your child, and you have a right to know.

Are you thinking, *of course I would listen if the teacher said my child needed help?* You'd be surprised by how many parents don't want to hear that their child is not excelling in school. I am not a psychiatrist, and I cannot possibly explain sticking your head in the sand when it comes to bad news about your children. Well, maybe I do understand that as parents we only want to see, hear and believe the best about our children, but the sooner a reading problem is acknowledged, the faster it can be solved. If the teacher tells you that your child is not reading at grade-level, *thank them*, and ask, "What's the plan?"

If you've picked up this book, you probably feel that your child needs some extra help in reading. That's good enough for me, and it should be for you, too. But, if you want more than a gut feeling to help you decide whether or not your child needs reading help, there are a few places you can look:

Homework

Does your child often have trouble understanding and completing homework assignments? Is she able to read and understand the directions? In most cases, homework is a review of lessons taught in school that day; a quick glance should be all that's needed to remind your child what needs to be done. While one would expect a student to have homework issues periodically, confusion and struggles night after night are red flags.

Spelling Tests

Most elementary school spelling programs teach new words by grouping those with a common phonetic feature (chain, rain, stain, maintain). The words are introduced to students at the beginning of the week, reviewed frequently in class and given again in homework assignments. If your child still has trouble reading and spelling these words by Friday's test, Houston, we have a problem.

Grades

Take a look at your child's report cards. Search as far back as you can. I have seen parents shocked to learn that their child was not reading at grade level. "We had no idea," they tell me. Yet, when we look in the child's cumulative file, which should have copies of previous report cards, we find that a reading problem has *existed* for years. What grades has your child been getting? Anything lower than a B (or a 3 on a scale of 4) implies lack of mastery.

Fluency Rate

In a nutshell, fluency is reading speed and accuracy. Fluency is a crucial component to reading, and we will discuss it in depth in later chapters. Many school districts have begun to require that the fluency rate (the number of correct words read in a minute) be noted on report cards. I am pleased when this information is shared, but it is only helpful to parents if they know what the number should be for their child's particular grade. For example, a fluency rate of 95 words per minute is cause for celebration when your child is in the 1st grade and not such good news four years later.

Test Scores

I strongly believe there is an overreliance on testing, especially in elementary education. Millions of our children are given norm-referenced tests which, by definition, must be scored so that *half* the testing population scores *below* 50% (Fair Test). What kind of test is designed so that half the children must fail? Norm-referenced tests are constantly changed (usually made harder) to maintain the half-above, half-below results. This is just one of many, many reasons why I am not a great fan of standardized testing. That being said, these tests *can* help you determine whether or not your child needs to be tutored in reading. Whether or not one believes that a particular test is too hard, a score *substantially* below 50% means that a child is reading far below his peers.

Attitude

Does your child like to read? Her attitude about reading can tell you a lot. Your daughter may prefer TV or video games or talking on the phone to reading (we are going to work on changing that!), and that's okay. One needs to be concerned about the child that HATES to read, never wants to read, has never picked up a book or magazine for pleasure. If she's never been interested in Harry Potter or Junie B. Jones or the million other children's book series that seem to be publicized everywhere...something's going on. We all gravitate towards things that are easy and fun for us; we avoid those things that are difficult or laborious. Children are no different. If reading is easy for them, they like to read. If it is a struggle, they do not enjoy it and try to get out of doing it, both in the classroom and at home. If your child would rather clean the garage and wash windows than read, she probably needs tutoring in reading.

I will say that sometimes a child may be a good reader but has not been *sold* on reading. Tragically, they have never come across a book that piques their interest more than drawing or skateboarding or Nickelodeon. If your child falls into this category, rejoice! You now have the opportunity to explore all of the superb children's literature out there today! We will cover this in ***Chapter 12 How to Teach Fluency Lessons***.

You have looked at weekly spelling tests, studied old and new report cards, spoken to the teacher, noticed that your son or daughter never reads on his or her own, and felt *that feeling*. You know that your child probably needs help in reading. Don't despair! In my experience, most children that are below grade-level in reading are only missing a few pieces of the reading puzzle. A few key concepts have been missed, and so the whole reading picture is unclear. Once these concepts are mastered, everything comes into focus. Understand that the earlier reading intervention takes place, the easier and more likely it is for your child to catch up. In the second grade, a reading problem is a reading problem; in the eighth grade, it is a social studies, language arts, math and science problem.

I once heard an analogy that clearly explained what happens when a child falls behind in reading. Imagine a group of children as trains in a train station on parallel tracks (stay with me). In the beginning, say kindergarten, all the trains are lined up next to one another. For the most part, everybody is at the same place in the race to learn how to read. The year progresses and most children move down the track at a nice, steady pace. Although a child might fall behind a little bit, the difference between trains can easily be made up with a little extra effort. But as the years pass- 1ˢᵗ grade, 2ⁿᵈ grade, 3ʳᵈ grade- the trains not only continue moving forward, they pick up speed. Instead of one or two train lengths between children, *miles and miles* separate the trains at the front and back of the pack. The trains in front are flying down the track, and it will take great effort and a lot of time to catch them now. Some of the trains have been behind for so long that they have become discouraged and lost hope of ever catching up to the other trains, much less be in the head of the pack.

This powerful analogy has remained with me because it clearly illustrates a common phenomenon and underscores the seriousness of stepping in as early as possible and doing whatever it takes to help your child become a powerful reader.

Please don't think that you must be a professional reading specialist with an advanced degree to tutor your child in reading. You don't. The first step is determining exactly where your child is having difficulty; then, you can zero in and solve the problem.

Let's begin, shall we?

CHAPTER 2

HOW CHILDREN LEARN TO READ

You have decided to tutor your child. Great decision! This is the perfect time to learn how children actually learn to read. Relax! You don't need a Masters degree, and what follows is by no means a complete explanation on the subject. A rudimentary understanding of how children read is more than enough for you to help your child improve. This chapter will quickly explain how children learn and the Big Three components of reading. If your child is struggling, you will have an idea of why and what you can do to remedy the situation. You will also be better able to work with teachers and reading specialists.

We often take our ability to read for granted, but it is truly an amazing feat. Just ask animals. Learning to read is a complex and lengthy process. Ideally, the steps begin to take place long before a child starts school- or even begins talking. Despite that exciting moment when your five year-old sees the letters and yells, "CAT!" no one learns to read instantaneously. It happens gradually over time. Most parents naturally encourage and support children as they move through each stage. Give yourself a pat on the back if you have ever read a book to a small child, put magnetic letters on your refrigerator or listened to nonsense rhymes *ad nauseum*. These are just some of the ways that parents help their children move through the five stages of learning to read.

Five Stages of Learning to Read

1. *Phonological Awareness* occurs when a child becomes aware of sounds. Dara understands that *sss* is a sound! She is delighted to hiss like a snake for hours on end, much to her parents' delight and annoyance.

2. Phonemes are the smallest bits of sound, smaller even than syllables and are usually represented by letters. *Phonemic Awareness* occurs when a child understands that sounds have symbols or letters that represent them. Dara

realizes that *s* represents the *sss* sound. She writes *s* on paper, in books, on the walls...

3. **Knowledge of Alphabetic Principles** occurs when a child discovers that words are made up of symbols or letters. Dara sees the *s* in the word *sat* and knows that *pan* has a *p* in it.

4. **Orthographic Awareness** occurs when the child realizes that writing has meaning and structure. Letters make up words; words make up sentences; and sentences tell stories. Dara opens her favorite book and understands that the words on the page tell the story.

5. Finally, **Reading** takes place when Dara recognizes words and understands their meaning. She's reading!

Or, to put it more simply,

There are **sounds**.
Those sounds are made up of **symbols (letters)**.
Symbols are put together to make **words**.
Words are put together to make **sentences**.
Recognition and understanding of the symbols, words and sentences
is **reading**.

Reading is interpreting symbols. It is a little bit more complicated than that, but unless you are an educator or a politician seeking re-election as the Education Candidate, you have probably had no reason to know any of this. In fact, you don't need to become a reading expert now. <u>Tutor Your Child to Reading Success</u> *does* assume that your child knows all of the letters and their corresponding sounds. If your child is an early or limited reader, you will need to review the alphabet with him until he has mastered letter-sound correlation. Be aware that some letters and their sounds are more difficult to learn than others (h, l, m, n, q, r, w, y). Other letters look alike (b and d, p and q) and are easy to confuse. Some letters have sounds that are easy to confuse (c and k, c and s).

Do you remember a few years ago when everybody was talking about computers and technology and the digital divide? One hardly hears anything about it anymore. It's taken for granted that in this technological world, we all need to be computer-literate. These days, reading is the hot topic. If you want to cause a ruckus, say, "Reading test scores!" at a school board meeting. It's like yelling, "Fire!" in a crowded theater. Test scores are the markers by which teachers, schools, principals, school districts and even states are judged. If reading scores improve, you have promotions, extra funding, balloons and smiles all around. If reading scores remain the same or drop, it is viewed as a crushing failure, and the finger pointing begins.

I believe that the emphasis on scores, scores, scores is hurting our children, but the insanity can sometimes be a blessing in disguise. Never has more information been available about the science of reading: how children read, why some children have difficulty learning to read, and what educators can do to help. Politicians and school districts are spending millions of dollars to fund reading research. Before you thank and kiss your government representatives, understand that they are probably not supporting these studies because they dream of seeing your son happily reading Charlotte's Web. Their primary concern is raising reading test scores this year...and next year...and the year after that.

My cynicism is based on experience. At one school it was decided that due to budget cuts, before-school tutoring would only be available on a limited basis. It was unfortunate, but despite overwhelming need, only a small number of students would be able to receive extra help. Teachers were told to choose five students from each class to receive this extra tutoring. Naturally, teachers wanted to send those students that were the farthest behind and needed the most help. No such luck. Teachers were required to study standardized test scores and choose five students *that were close to moving up into a higher category or about to drop into a lower category.* It didn't matter if a student was doing fabulously or poorly; the most important thing was to push anyone that could be pushed up, and stop anybody from falling down. Those students whose reading fell in the middle of a lower category were not considered a good use of funds. It was unlikely that their reading scores would improve and put them into a higher category, and there was no lower category for them to fall into. They wouldn't help the school or district look any better or make it look any worse, so why give them extra help? This meant that George, who was reading in the middle of the Far Below Basic category, stayed at home while Ruben received help to move from Proficient to Highly Proficient. Improving test score at the expense of children should not be tolerated, and, years later it still astounds me.

The one and only consolation to this type of foolishness is that in the desire to improve test scores, more and more reading studies are being funded. Politics is an ugly business, but I will take the information any way I can get it.

Despite the interest in how children learn to read, there is no general consensus as to the best way to teach them. This should come as no surprise when you understand that since the mid-19th century, there has been an ongoing debate between two major camps as to the best way to teach children to read. While the words used to describe these reading opponents have changed throughout the years, their basic philosophies and arguments have, remarkably, changed very little. Basically, on one side we have those who believe that **phonics** is the superior reading method and on the other side we find those who feel a **whole language** approach is best. At any given time, one philosophy is more popular (accepted) than the other.

When I began teaching, everybody was supposedly using whole language. Teaching phonics was considered old-fashioned, and only dinosaurs tried to push phonics onto their poor students. Teachers who persisted in teaching phonics were forced to use their old books and yellowed mimeographed worksheets from the 70s, or create materials. There simply weren't any new phonics materials to be found. Whole Language ruled the world.

There was one problem: a lot of kids couldn't read. Test scores were abysmal, teachers were stunned, parents were outraged, politicians started stuttering. It was time for the reading pendulum to swing, as it always does, back the other way. Researchers began to grudgingly admit that there might be a very small place for phonics in an elementary classroom. Those formerly "crazy" phonics teachers began to come out of the closet, mumbling something about reading success. I knew things were changing when I was given the book Phonics for Older Students by my principal. I thought, "Great! We'll be able to use *both* whole language and phonics!" It seemed obvious to me even then that a mixture of phonics and whole language would be better than an either-or approach.

There are those who believe the reading pendulum is now in the middle, somewhere between whole language and phonics. The new catch phrase is *balanced instruction*, a perfect mixture of phonics and whole language. Don't believe the hype. Most reading instruction is still *either* phonics or whole language, not both. Thousands of teachers were raised on a diet of whole language and would rather starve than eat phonics. Also, few teachers have been trained to teach both whole language and phonics, so they use whichever method they have always used.

Whether or not you were taught to read using phonics or whole language depends on your age and where the imaginary pendulum happened to be at the time. You might have been one of the fortunate few that had a teacher willing and able to incorporate both whole language and phonics into his or her curriculum, but that is rare. Most teachers are taught one philosophy in teacher training school and pushed, pushed, pushed to follow the crowd. The good news is that 80% of children will learn how to read no matter which style is taught. Consider that within that 80%, there are many, many students that have learned to read, but the process was not nearly as easy as it could have been if they had been taught both phonics and whole language. We end up with children that *can* read, but they didn't enjoy learning to do it.

By this point you must be wondering what the difference is between phonics and whole language, anyway.

The Difference Between Whole Language and Phonics

Whole language proponents believe that reading happens naturally, and to teach reading directly is counter-intuitive. Adults don't get on the floor to teach babies to crawl, do they? Of course not; babies do it naturally and intuitively. In that same vein, whole language proponents believe that humans are hard-wired to read, and children will learn to read if teachers simply provide the right environment and get out of the way. Whole language teachers believe that direct phonics instruction (sound-letter correlation, sounding out words, blending letters into sounds, spelling and punctuation) is boring and unnecessary. Studying individual words and learning how to read them out of context is a waste of time and can actually hamper reading acquisition (Moats, Cromwell). Why force students to learn these things when they will pick it all up on their own?

In whole language classrooms, students are taught to use context clues such as looking at pictures and thinking about what would make sense if they come across a word they don't know. The idea is that if students are adequately exposed to print in a fun, exciting and "authentic" environment, they will learn how to read and spell easily and independently.

The phonics people disagree, of course. They claim that common sense and research have proven time and again that reading is NOT a natural process, but one that must be taught with thorough, systematic and direct instruction. In the long history of human development, reading and writing are the new kids on the block. We may be hard-wired to speak to one another, but creating symbols to represent the sounds we make, combining those symbols to represent the words we speak, recognizing those words on a piece of parchment...none of it comes easily or naturally.

Unlike their whole language counterparts, phonics proponents don't believe that children learn to read by imitating adults as they do with spoken language. It is ridiculous, according to the phonics people, to expect children to pick up reading through imitation. One does not need to know phonics during a spoken conversation, but sounding out or decoding words is a crucial skill when learning how to read. The ability to read any word- even those you have never seen or heard before- without relying on outside clues is the initial goal of phonics. Automatic decoding means that children don't have to look at pictures and other clues to figure out what is going on. Once children have gained context-free word recognition, they will be able to read with greater speed and comprehension. Phonics teachers use classroom time to directly and repeatedly teach phonics, syllabication, spelling patterns and grammar rules.

I believe that children need a balance of phonics and whole language to learn best. When children are learning to read in kindergarten and 1st grade, they need a lot of phonics. Teachers must show students how to decode unknown words so time and energy are not lost looking for clues to guess meaning. As children become better decoders, whole language methods should naturally constitute a larger part of the reading curriculum, although I believe that there is always a place for phonics. Let's call it *word attack skills* for the big kids.

We could spend years trying to figure out why so many children have trouble reading, but I choose to rely on my experience as a student, teacher and tutor working with students from 2ⁿᵈ through 8ᵗʰ grades. ***Nearly all of the students reading below grade level in the upper grades did not receive enough (or any) phonics instruction in the lower grades.*** I am not including children with reading disabilities, although many of them could be included in that category, as well.

There are a number of reasons why a child did not receive enough phonics instruction. Perhaps he had a teacher that didn't believe in phonics and taught whole language. Perhaps there was a strong phonics program in place, but the child just needed more review. Maybe the student was absent or moved frequently. (I once had a 5ᵗʰ grade student tell me that she hadn't been to school since 2ⁿᵈ grade because she needed to stay home to "keep Mama company." I don't need to tell you that this poor child was not reading anywhere near grade-level, do I?) It is certainly maddening and frustrating to realize that your child didn't receive proper reading instruction, but, at certain point, it really doesn't make sense to look back. It is not going to change the fact that your child must now learn how to decode. Without this skill, reading will be a nightmare.

The Big Three

Phonics

Decoding (recognizing letter patterns and using them to sound out words) is a skill that, once learned, should become virtually automatic. Good readers know that *tion* sounds like *shun*, but they do not actively have to think about the rule while reading. Imagine how frustrating reading would be if you were stumped each and *every* time you came across the words action, *investigation, lotion,* etc. What a notion!

Until now, you have probably not thought about the hundreds of decoding skills you know and use. Once your child learns phonics rules, they can forget them, too. Rules will become part of their automatic decoding arsenal, and they will decode and read almost without thinking.

You may be wondering why teachers don't take time and review phonics rules with those students that need it. The problem is often one of time. Teaching (and learning) phonics is not difficult, but it does take time. In the lower grades (K-3) time may be allotted for phonics instruction, but by the 4th grade, there is very little time to devote to it. Upper grade teachers have incredible amounts of information to cover in all subjects- and hardly any time to go back and *reteach* anything. There is also another problem, a philosophy called Learning to Read/ Reading to Learn.

Learning to Read/ Reading to Learn is based on the assumption that instruction in the lower grades focuses on teaching a child *how* to read, and instruction in the upper grades focuses on learning new content (Robb). For example, in the third grade a teacher shows Johnny how to decode the word *electricity*; in the fourth grade the teacher expects Johnny to be able to read about the properties of electricity in his science book. The problem with the Learning to Read/ Reading to Learn is that many children still need direct reading instruction in the intermediate and upper grades. A first grader may have a reading problem, but an eighth grader has problems in reading, math, science, social studies...

Oh well, there is no reason to sit on your hands wondering if your child's teacher will find the time and inclination to review phonics. We will cover phonics in depth in *Chapter 7 How to Give Phonics Assessments* and *Chapter 11 How to Teach Phonics Lessons*.

Sight Words

When I was in the 1st grade, my mother decided that I wasn't reading as well as I should. To this day she is unable to remember or explain exactly what lead her to this conclusion. My teacher said I was doing fine, but my mother, relying on her intuition, decided to take matters into her own hands. Every day after school I would change my school clothes, eat a quick snack and sit down to practice reading with my mother. We didn't have a special program to follow. My mother would simply open one of my books and ask me to read. If I came to a word that I didn't know and *couldn't sound out*, my mother would tell me the word and ask me to repeat it. Occasionally, this is all it would take, and I would know the word the next time I saw it. The words that caused me the most trouble were those that I could not sound out. These words are called *sight words*.

Sight words are the most commonly spoken and written words in the English language. We call them sight words because a reader needs to recognize these words on sight. Readers come across these words constantly, and need to read them quickly and automatically. It is amazing how often we see the same words while reading. Children's literature, especially, is chock-full of sight words. Depending on whom you ask, sight words make up 60%-85% of the words in children's reading material. In the lowest grades, you will sometimes find *80% of all the words in a book or a story are sight words*. Wow! That's almost *every* word on a page. If a child does not know 80% of the words they see, and have no way of figuring them out- who would blame them for giving up in frustration? What a colossal waste of time it would be to stop *every* time you saw a sight word!

Besides the fact that sight words are so prevalent in our children's reading, there are two other reasons why sight words must be memorized. First of all, while some sight words can be decoded, many cannot. Used constantly over the years, these words have become bastardized- they no longer sound the way they once did. Hundreds of years ago people said "come" like "comb," but nobody says it that way anymore- unless they are really strange. Many sight words have silent letters, or follow strange phonics rules that are no longer part of modern English. The frustrating thing is that while the pronunciation of sight words has changed, the spelling has remained the same.

The words no longer sound like they look; trying to decode them is useless.

Another problem with sight words is that many are taken from other languages, and one can't use English phonics to sound out non-English words. For example, the sight word *beautiful* comes from the French word *beau*. We do not typically use the letter combination of *eau* in English. And, even if we do know that *eau* sounds like *o* in French, we don't pronounce the word like that, anyway!

Don't misunderstand, I like sight words. They bring people together. Sight words may be the only subject in which phonics and whole language folks come together in peace and harmony. Readers don't use decoding strategies (phonics) or context clues (whole language) to read sight words. Everybody agrees that the only way to learn sight words is to memorize them- and the earlier the better.

Sight words are sometimes called different things. Various organizations publish their own sight word lists. One of the most commonly-used lists is the Dolch List. There isn't much debate as to which words are the most common in our language; the difference lies in how to group and teach the words. For example, one organization believes a word should be learned in 1st grade, another says it's a 2nd grade word. Most of the sight words lists in Tutor Your Child to Reading Success come from 300 Instant Words by Elizabeth Sakiey and Edward Fry (Jamestown, 1984)and also include words not always found on other lists such as colors and days of the week. Your primary concern when teaching sight words is that they are common, high-frequency words. Don't waste your time with lists that are based upon only one story or book. There is no point in asking your child to memorize special words from one story. Teach her those words that are going to be found in *most* of the books she will read.

Getting back to my afternoon reading sessions with my mother... Although it felt like a lifetime to a six year-old, my mother and I only studied sight words for a few months. One day she decided that I knew what I was supposed to know, and we no longer had our little afternoon tutoring sessions. Thank goodness that my mother took charge of her child's reading instruction and did not wait a few years for a teacher to say I was hopelessly behind.

You'll become *very* familiar with sight words in **Chapter 6 How to Give Sight Word Assessments** and **Chapter 10 How to Teach Sight Word Lessons**.

Fluency

The next member of the Big Three in Reading is *fluency*. Fluency is the development of *reading speed after accuracy*. Fluency is often misunderstood. Some people think being a fluent reader only means being a fast reader. Fluent readers do more than read quickly; they read accurately with few or no errors. Fluent readers read with intonation, meaning they stress the right words, pause at commas, stop at periods, and raise their voices when asking a question. They know that they are reading to an audience and telling a story - not just speed reading. Fluent readers understand what they are reading, and it sounds like it. John Shefelbine of The Developmental Studies Center says that the fluent reader sounds good, is easy to listen to, and reads with enough expression to help the listener understand and enjoy the material.

The ultimate purpose of reading is comprehension, and it is important to understand that fluency and comprehension go hand-in-hand. **You read well when you understand what you are reading. You understand what you are reading when you read well.** It's the chicken-egg thing.

I was once required in a teacher training class to read a paragraph from an industrial science manual (fun class). The material was incredibly technical and totally unfamiliar. I was able to decode *every* word, but I could not read with much feeling and intonation because I had no idea what it was about. On top of that, by the end of the paragraph I had totally forgotten what I had read in the beginning! This exercise was amusing and enlightening, but I cannot imagine living like that *every* day. Who wants to read without understanding?

I have a sad story that illustrates how entwined fluency and comprehension are. My very first year teaching, I had a lovely student named "Ella" in my 4th/5th grade class. Ella had amazing decoding skills; she could read almost *anything* you put in front of her. She read quickly and accurately, but her reading was missing the other components of fluency- feeling, inflection and expression. It was painfully obvious that Ella didn't *feel* the story. Her reading was boring and flat, and hearing her read gave me my first clue that Ella probably understood very little of what she read. My suspicions were confirmed when Ella was unable to relate any of the pertinent information (who, what, when, where or how) of what she had just finished reading. It was heartbreaking.

Ella's situation was extreme (we later found out that she had serious developmental issues), but we can learn something from it. Ella could read nearly all of the words on a page- many children aren't even able to do that- but still did not understand what she had read. Imagine the child that spends five minutes stumbling through a paragraph- how much information can she possibly remember? Anything?

If a child is not reading at grade level, somebody had better figure out how to teach sight words, phonics, and fluency. Only after mastering all three can a child become a good reader- or even one that loves to read! This includes children with mild reading disabilities.

Reading Disabilities

I include a very short description of three of the most common learning disabilities as described by Delaware Community College's Reading Department website article, *Common Reading Disabilities*. This general information is for those parents that have a feeling that something is going on. You cannot determine whether or not your child has a learning disability by reading this book. ***Please consult with a trained professional for a proper diagnosis***.

Attention Deficit Disorder (ADD; ADHD includes hyperactivity) is a disability in which a child may have problems focusing, sitting still, concentrating, dealing with distractions, finishing tasks and assignments, getting along and working with others, understanding abstract ideas and details, following directions, and multi-tasking (doing more than one thing at a time). All or some of these symptoms might be present. There are many different theories about the causes of ADD an ADHD. ADD is treated either with drugs, behavior modifications or a combination of the two.

Imagine how difficult it would be to learn to read if you had ADD! Despite your greatest effort and best intention, you would experience difficulty listening and concentrating. Lessons, directions and instructions would often be missed. On top of everything, your behavior, through no fault of your own, would often get you into trouble.

Dysgraphia is a learning disability that results from a disorder in the part of the brain that controls writing. A student suffering from dysgraphia will often have illegible writing and other problems in the areas of spelling, grammar, punctuation and sentence structure. Although dysgraphia is a disability that primarily affects writing, reading is usually compromised as well.

Dyslexia occurs in about 1% to 2% of the population. Remember phonemic awareness? People with dyslexia have difficulty distinguishing the individual sounds that make up words and so are missing the second, crucial step in reading development. Without direct phonemic instruction, they will be unlikely to move on to the next steps of reading acquisition.

All three of these learning disabilities are diagnosed through observation, and intelligence and learning tests. If you think that your child has one of these learning disabilities, do whatever it takes to get them tested, including bugging the teacher to bug whoever does the testing. Turn in all paperwork promptly, and make copies of everything. You might choose to pay for the tests yourself. Time is of the essence. Think about those trains rolling down the track. Every day, week, month, year that a child cannot read well takes them farther and farther away from the likelihood that they will ever love to read.

CHAPTER 3

FORMAL VS. INFORMAL TUTORING WORKING WITH TEACHERS

In <u>Tutor Your Child to Reading Success</u> parents are shown how to work with children during what I call *formal tutoring* sessions. You are not required to dress up during these sessions, unless you choose to, of course! Formal tutoring means tutoring that takes place during planned times with a specific, goal-oriented agenda. Helping our children become masterful readers requires a no-nonsense, direct approach, and it cannot be done on the fly. Carving out time in our packed schedules can be a challenge, but we must find regular, special and uninterrupted time to devote to phonics, sight words and fluency.

Informal Tutoring

Before we discuss formal tutoring and how to make time for it, I would like to share the many opportunities parents have throughout the day for *informal tutoring*. Informal tutoring occurs during those unplanned teachable moments that arise while we live our lives. It is sobering to realize that we are teaching our children *every* second that they are in our presence. Our children emulate our behavior- good and bad. They learn about the world and their place in it largely from observing us. More is *caught* than *taught*.

Teachable moments naturally take place in the classroom, but it is the un-expected learning that takes place at home that I find so powerful. In terms of reading, the best informal tutoring that our children will *ever* receive is seeing us read. We don't have to make a big announcement, "Look! I AM READ-ING!" Taking time to read a few pages of a book or a quick magazine article in front of our children speaks volumes.

Some parents wait to read until after the children are in bed. I do this, as well, and I am not asking parents to give it up. However, please try to read while the kids are awake, too! It is crucial for your children to see you reading for pleasure, even if only for a few minutes. Turn of the television for an hour tonight and join your children reading. After a few moans and groans, your children will realize that they can still live without the TV. You will be amazed by the quiet and peace in your home! Remember to use this time to read- not clean the kitchen or pay bills.

Another opportunity for informal tutoring takes place in the car. Cars, with doors and locks, make our children our captive audience. Use car time to your advantage! Turn off the radio (or TV), and get your children reading. If your children are able to read in the car without getting carsick, encourage them to do it. Even on short car rides, most of us pass hundreds of road signs, store signs, banners, etc. Read some of the signs out loud: *exit, toll, bridge, stop, cleaners, Jones' Market*. Before you know it, your child will know dozens of words. (Why do they always learn how to read the fast food restaurants signs first?)

Recently, I was driving behind a service van. I cannot tell you what service they provided, but I had no trouble reading the huge slogan on the back: "We Do It Right the First Time!" I wished that my four year old son had been with me. He is learning sight words, and would have been thrilled to read *it* and *the*! I am sure I could have added *we* and *do* to his sight word list!

I am no great fan of television, but it is a part of most families' daily lives, including mine. Instead of sitting there passively, soaking up all of the silliness, use the TV for informal tutoring. Watch TV with your children as often as you can stand it. Not only are you able to monitor and discuss what they watch, there are commercials! You don't like commercials? Why, with big, bold words, and catchy jingles repeated over and over and over again, commercials are great opportunities for informal tutoring! Don't get a snack during commercials, teach your children some new words! As words flash across the screen, read them out loud then ask your child to try. A favorite game of mine is How Do You Spell That? Choose a word or phrase from the commercial and ask your child to spell it. For example, you say, "How do you spell *cereal*?" Watch as your children search the commercial to find the word!

There are dozens of opportunities for informal tutoring. Be creative. When the phone rings, ask your son to read the name on the caller id screen. Challenge your daughter to read the newspaper headlines while you cook dinner. Give your son a dollar if he can alphabetize the spice rack. Let your daughter look at the mail; tell her that she can stay up five minutes past bedtime every time she finds a new return address city or state. Your son wants a special meal? If he reads the directions, you'll make it. The idea is to get your child to have fun reading!

Formal Tutoring

Let's get back to formal tutoring, the tutoring that you plan and make happen. While informal tutoring of some sort will hopefully continue throughout childhood, formal tutoring probably will not. How much time you devote to formal tutoring depends on your schedule and your child's individual needs, of course.

Parents are incredibly busy. Children, significant others, church, clubs, sports, jobs, housework, laundry- a myriad of responsibilities and interests take up our time and energy. And now I am telling you to make time for tutoring! It is true- for a short time, some activities may have to be put on the back burner. It's called prioritizing, and it's something adults must do. Whenever I tell myself that I am too busy to do what needs to be done, I remember reading that one of our past presidents managed to jog a few miles each morning. I may be busy, but there is no way I am busier than the President of the United States! If he can find an hour each day for exercise, what's my excuse?

My grandmother used to say that a person can do anything for a season and a reason, and what better reason for freeing up your evenings or weekends than helping your child become a good reader? Reading well is a gift that will last longer than next semester's report card or that dream job after college. Being a good, strong reader is something your child will have today, tomorrow, and for the rest of her life. Don't you want your child to have the freedom to pick up a newspaper and find out what is going on in the world or to open a book and learn whatever she wants to know? Curling up with a good book is one of life's best comforts- who would deny it to their children? New worlds await those who read. There are new friends to meet and new places to visit! Reading gives us so much: information, entertainment, an escape from life's daily toil and trouble.

Parents are no strangers to sacrifice and hard work. Yes, you might have to change your schedule while you tutor your child to reading success. Yes, tutoring is hard work- that's why people are paid to do it. But, tutoring your own child is the best kind of work, and the payment is immeasurable.

Just as there are major differences between running a daycare program and "watching kids," there are also a number of ways in which formal tutoring is different from helping with homework once in a while. By giving your tutoring sessions a place of importance in your life and making the sessions pleasant for those involved, both you and your child are much more likely to stay motivated to continue. In particular, I ask parents to carve out a specific time for tutoring sessions, find a quiet environment in which to tutor, and do their best to always have a positive attitude while tutoring.

Specific Time

How much time *should* you devote to tutoring? It is not always *easy* to strike a balance between spending enough time helping your child become a masterful reader and spending so much time tutoring that they become resistant and resentful. I have found that 45 minutes is the longest amount of time you should ask anybody to focus on a topic without a break. Adults are better at hiding it than children, but our minds wander and we lose focus, too. I recommend that tutoring sessions should last 30 to 45 minutes. Try spending 15 minutes on sight words, 15 minutes on phonics and 15 minutes on fluency. I guarantee that if you do this 4 or 5 times a week, you will be astounded by your child's reading progress.

You do not want to make a habit of skipping tutoring sessions, but tutoring is a waste of time if you and/or your child are ill or especially tired. We all have those hectic, busy days, but don't let them prevent you from tutoring. There might only be enough time for your son to read the sight words on the refrigerator or play a quick game of phonics Tic-Tac-Toe before bed, but *even* 10 minutes of review can be beneficial. Not *every* tutoring session has to be 45 minutes and formal.

Every family is unique. Perhaps you have more time and childcare options available on the weekends, and spend 45 minutes tutoring on Saturday and Sunday, but only manage to squeeze in a couple of 30 minute sessions during the week. Other families have jam-packed weekends and would rather tutor during the week. Do what works best for you and your family situation. **Be flexible, but remember, if you and your child put the time in now, you won't need to do this forever**.

Are you asking yourself, *where in the world am I going to find the time for tutoring?* Be creative. Get up a little early and take care of the chores that you usually do in the evening. Or, skip those chores altogether! Dishes, dust and dirty clothes can wait a little while! Don't sleep in so late on weekend mornings. Give up a half hour of nighttime TV or video games for a few months. Tell your friends that you will be helping your daughter with her reading, and those nightly telephone chat fests will now happen on the weekend. Cook and freeze some meals ahead and instead of making dinner, use that time for tutoring. Get a crock pot, and let dinner greet you in the evening. Open the mail and answer emails some other time.

You need to find time for tutoring, but be realistic. It doesn't make sense to say, "Ok, every night from 5 to 5:45, we're going to work on reading!" when you know good and well that's dinner time, and everybody is going to be starved and hollering.

Quiet Environment Free of Distractions

I strongly recommend finding a place other than your home for your tutoring sessions. Our homes have too many distractions- telephones, doorbells, laundry waiting to be folded. You may be able to somehow ignore the dust bunnies under the sofa and the light blinking on the answering machine, but your mental energy and focus will not be completely on your child where it needs to be. It is because of all of the distractions- two-legged, four-legged and inanimate- that I recommend taking your tutoring sessions outside of your house.

If you are able to afford it, hire a babysitter and get out of the house to watch your other children while you tutor. Your other children can occupy themselves while you tutor their brother or sister? I *still* caution you against tutoring at home. Your children have not been in the dining room since Thanksgiving, but as soon as you take their sister in there for tutoring, they find a million reasons to visit. Every little thing escalates into a major problem that must be shared with Mom and Dad, *immediately*. If my children know that I am anywhere in the house or garage, they will find me and ask me bizarre questions or scream at the top of their lungs so that I feel compelled to find them. They won't leave me alone for a five minute phone call; how can I expect them to give me half an hour?

Some of you are thinking that your spouse or significant other can watch the kids while you tutor. Sure. Your spouse agrees to hold down the fort for 30 minutes while you tutor with your daughter. That's the plan, but the next thing you know, the baby is screaming, your spouse has forgotten how to fix a bottle, and you are no longer tutoring.

The child you are tutoring needs 100% of your attention for those 30 to 45 minutes. Get out of the house and away from everything that prevents you from devoting all of your energy to him.

Finding a quiet environment for tutoring doesn't have to cost you any money. Most public libraries have study rooms or areas where you can talk quietly.

Local recreation centers will often let you use their facilities. Do you know anybody with an office or conference room you can borrow a few times a week? Maybe one of your friends will give you the key to their house and you can tutor while they are at work. Ask around! People are more than happy to help.

Coffee shops can be great places for tutoring. They have tables and chairs, and good lighting. Most places don't care how long you stay. Plus, you can eat and read at the same time- two of my favorite pastimes! My daughter and I love to go to coffee shops. I work on the computer and sip delicious coffee while my daughter does her homework with hot chocolate or a cookie.

Bookstores are another option for tutoring outside of your home. Many bookstores, especially the large chains, now have cozy cafes as well as plenty of reading areas. Tutor your child while surrounded by thousands of books. Talk about good tutoring vibes!

I recommend scoping out a number of places before you actually begin tutoring. Choose two or three places that you find acceptable, and then bring your child to see them. Ask her which places she would like to try first. The more choices and ownership you give your daughter in regards to her tutoring, the more positive and cooperative she will be.

If you are unable or unwilling to tutor outside of your home, don't despair. The point is to really focus on your child and nothing else. Do your best to create a quiet, peaceful environment, even if you are at home. Turn of the TV, let the answering machine pick up the phone, and find a room with the least amount of traffic.

Positive Attitude

Hopefully, you are excited about tutoring your child, and you are doing it willingly because you love your child and want the best for him. Studies show that not only do good readers have better grades and higher self-esteem than poor readers, good readers are *perceived* by themselves and others to be smarter than poor readers in *all* areas. This means that even if your child is musically gifted, if he can't read well, he still might not think much of himself. It is sad, but not surprising. Children spend thousands of hours in classrooms where they either excel or struggle, and are subtly rewarded or punished for their reading abilities day after day, year after year. If a child constantly feels that they don't measure up, and can't do what *everybody else* can seemingly do, is it any wonder that they feel inferior?

As parents we try to combat all of the negativity that our children absorb at school. We must make a concerted effort to tutor our children with patience, love and understanding. It is not always easy, believe me. I know from experience how hard it is to put on a smile after a long day. You are tired, your child is tired, and nobody wants to talk about long vowel sounds. This is when you have to really work hard at being patient and positive. Try not to sigh loudly, look exasperated, or complain about tutoring. Don't yell at your child for forgetting a word they knew five minutes ago. If you simply cannot put on a happy face, stop tutoring. Say something honest like, "Whew! I am having a hard time today! Do you mind if we end a little early?" Your son will appreciate your honesty and no doubt be relieved. Who wants to feel like a burden? Finally, try to end all of your tutoring sessions on a positive note. In this way, your son will feel like a winner and look forward to the next time. You can say, "Good job! You've learned those words! Ready to go?"

In all of my years teaching and tutoring, I have never come across a child that wanted to be a poor reader. Not one. Ever. They all want to do well and make the adults in their lives- especially Mom and Dad- proud of them. Try to be patient with them. Have fun, even! If you do a good job now, perhaps your children will read to you in your old age.

Teachers

Parents often ask me about working with teachers. I believe that open dialogue between parents and teachers can only benefit children. With this in mind, I want to caution you against thinking that teachers have all the answers concerning your child's academic needs.

Our society likes to put teachers on a pedestal. We don't like to pay them once they're *on* the pedestal, but we want them up there, nonetheless. We have an idea that all teachers are wonderful, selfless, and do nothing but think about their students. Teachers do go home, but only long enough to rest and change their clothes. They would rather be at school teaching; it's what they live for. I am being facetious, but the fact is that teachers are expected to be exceptional human beings. Unlike the rest of us, teachers aren't supposed to make mistakes, get fed-up or give up. Most of the teachers I have met and worked with have been sacrificing, hard-working, and loving individuals that want to make a difference in children's lives. They certainly didn't become teachers for the money! On the other hand, some of the teachers I have met and worked with have been petty, lazy and mean. Some have been a combination. Most teachers have good and bad days, even good and bad years. The reality is that teachers are people- they have different personalities, histories, working conditions, and personal issues. One cannot, across the board, expect all teachers to be the same. This sounds obvious, but I don't know how many times I've heard, "My older son's teacher did such-and-such!" or "When I was in the 5ᵗʰ grade, we learned it this way!" Accept that teachers are individuals. It will make your life- and theirs- much easier.

I've already said it, but it bears repeating- teachers are being asked to do more and more and more *every year*. Many teachers are simply tired and overworked. Your child's teacher may truly want to give your child extra, one-on-one attention but simply not have the time to do it. It's reality.

One of the most shocking things I found as a new teacher was that some of my students were reading two, three, even four years below grade level. Helping a child close this gap requires a lot of time and extra work, and the more people involved, the better. Let your teacher know that you are concerned about your child's reading, you are going to start a tutoring program, and you'd appreciate any help, suggestions, ideas, materials and recommendations that he can give you. Ask if your child has been receiving any extra help in class. Find out if any volunteers are available to read with your child during the day. Ask about tutoring programs offered by the school. Don't be shy, and don't wait for the teacher to contact you.

Busy or not, good teachers want to hear from parents. Say, "Mr. Gomez, I've been noticing that Bobby is having trouble reading his homework. I am going to start working with him. Do you have any suggestions?" After Mr. Gomez gets off the floor from a dead faint, he is likely to react in one of three ways:

1. Thrilled and Helpful. He's had dreams about parents saying what you have just said! This teacher would love for you to work with your child at home, and he can tell you Bobby's strengths and areas of concern. Listen to this teacher! Write down everything he says. You may choose to use or ignore his advice, but at least you will have heard his professional opinion. Take any materials that Mr. Gomez gives you and say, "Thanks!" Set up a time to get back with him to discuss progress, improvement, questions and any concerns.

2. Doubtful and Cautious. Mr. Gomez is from Missouri, the Show Me State. He would like nothing better than to believe that you are going to work hard

and tutor your child in reading, but he's seen excited parents before. He figures that you will get tired of tutoring before any real progress is made. Mr. Gomez isn't familiar with your commitment to your child or Tutor Your Child to Reading Success. Once your child's reading level and attitude improve, Mr. Gomez will become your biggest ally, but he wants to see some proof.

3. Opposed and Unhelpful. Be prepared for those teachers that believe parents should leave academic instruction to the professionals- teachers. Mr. Gomez is offended and affronted by the assumption that you think you can do his job, and he wonders what you've been doing all along. Don't expect applause or much help. Write down whatever he says, thank him and be on your way. Even when your child's reading improves, this teacher will be reluctant to give you- or this book- any credit.

I once worked with a teacher, let's call her Irene, that allowed a horrible experience in one school to affect how she interacted with students, parents and administrators for the rest of her teaching career. Irene's initial problem was her principal. The principal wanted to hire some of her friends as teachers, and decided to get rid of some existing staff to make room. Irene was one of the teachers on the principal's hit list. The principal used many unconscionable tactics to drive Irene out of the school, but the one that traumatized Irene the most was claiming that parents were complaining about her teaching methods. The principal intuited that if she kept getting calls and visits from unsatisfied parents, there would be no way to recommend Irene be re-hired the next year. The principal refused to tell Irene who was complaining or show her any letters, if they existed at all, which is doubtful. To this day, Irene becomes upset when she talks about that year. She was constantly on edge in her classroom, afraid to say anything to her students because they might misunderstand or twist what she said and tell their parents. She was a nervous wreck in and out of the classroom. Conferences, phone calls, any communication with parents, were a nightmare for Irene. She constantly wondered if she was talking to an undercover, dissatisfied parent.

The principal's harassment worked; Irene chose to leave that school. She was lucky enough to find a position the next year at a great school with a fabulous principal, but the damage was done. Irene knows that her former principal was probably making up complaints against her, but she is not certain. That uncertainty has made her incredibly wary and suspect of parents (and principals). She second-guesses herself constantly, and never relaxes with students or their parents. If you were to approach Irene and say that you thought your child needed reading help and wanted to know what Irene had been doing about it, she would react defensively. She would be convinced that you held her fully responsible and blamed her completely. You would not get much help from Irene because she would be too busy having a breakdown and waiting for the ax to fall.

This true story is just one example of why a teacher may be uncooperative with you and your tutoring plans. Teachers are individuals, and book bags aren't the only baggage they bring into the classroom. In no way do I excuse Irene's paranoia, but it's a reality for her students and their parents.

If your child is lucky enough to have a teacher with the time, energy, experience, inclination and skill to work with you while you are tutoring your child in reading, consider yourself very, very lucky. Understand, though, that you can help your child become a good, strong reader- grade-level and beyond- without the teacher's help. Regardless of what your child's teacher says or how they react, proceed with the steps in this book as planned.

CHAPTER **4**

GETTING STARTED AND HOW TO USE THIS BOOK

Are you ready to start tutoring your child to reading success? Please do yourself a favor and read this entire book at least once before you start. I know, I have been pushing parents to start tutoring now! Time is of the *essence!* The trains are moving down the track! Now, I am telling you to wait. While it *is* imperative to begin tutoring as soon as you suspect your child needs it, you don't want to move *too* quickly and risk being unprepared. One of the fastest ways to lose a student's interest is to lose momentum and have to stop, look for lost materials, or run to the copy machine. This is one of the very first lessons I learned in teacher training, and it has held me in good stead. Reading <u>Tutor Your Child to Reading Success</u> from cover to cover will ensure that you know exactly how to set up your tutoring plan. Take this time to be prepared.

You won't be doing formal tutoring forever, but while you are doing it, make it as convenient and organized as possible. Being organized will make your life a lot easier, which in turn will make your child's tutoring a lot easier. I strive to be organized, and in this book I show you how to set up a tutoring system that is both portable and organized. My first piece of advice is to keep everything you need for tutoring in one place, perhaps a tote bag or back pack. When you say, "Let's go to the coffee shop and do some reading!" you can grab the bag and be on your way. Too many projects in our lives get dropped simply because we are not organized. Who wants to search and hunt for materials and supplies every time they need them? I certainly don't, and I am assuming that you don't, either.

I believe in saving money, and many of the materials that I recommend are probably lying around your home office. If you can afford it, though, I strongly suggest that you buy new tutoring supplies. The materials and supplies listed here can be found at most office supply stores, big box stores, drugstores, and even a few supermarkets. You probably won't have to spend more than $5 or $10, but the payoff could be huge if you make a big deal out of letting your child pick out some things. Not only is shopping fun, you are making it clear that something big is taking place. Tutoring is special and exciting. Show your child that helping her become a good reader is important to you, and you are willing to put your money where your mouth is, so to speak.

Nothing gets me in the mood for learning faster than sharp pencils and a new notebook! Each September I buy these things for myself simply because it feels like a new school year, and I am ready to move on to the next grade! If you are able, take your child to the store to buy at least a few new supplies. It's a relatively inexpensive way to create a feeling of newness about reading.

You know your financial situation better than I do, of course, so do what is best for you and your family.

Besides a few pencils, pens and crayons, I recommend the following:

3-Ring Binder (2 inch or greater)

I love 3-Ring binders! I use them for almost every project. You will be making and storing *a lot* of copies, and I strongly suggest that you put everything into one binder. Think of your binder as Tutoring Command Central. Get one that is sturdy and will last. Buy cheap, buy twice. They cost a few dollars more, but I especially like those binders with clear plastic pockets on the front and back. Your child can draw a picture to decorate and personalize his tutoring binder. The outside pockets are also good places to keep tutoring information easily accessible. Three hole-punched tab dividers can be labeled and also keep your binder organized.

If you choose not to use a 3-Ring Binder, get a heavy-duty pocket folder.

Clear Page Protectors

Page protectors are indispensable for keeping originals neat and clean. I also recommend using them to hold flash cards and other light supplies. Be sure to get the kind that are three hole-punched so that they can be used with your binder.

Removable Tabs

Removable tabs are those little sticky flags that help you mark your place in a book. I use these things everywhere because they help you find your place in a book, magazine or stack of papers quickly and easily.

Children's Dictionary

Your child needs a good children's dictionary for homework, research projects, reports, tutoring, and life. Looking up an unknown word in the dictionary is almost a guaranteed method for learning it. If you plan on using your adult dictionary to save a few dollars, *please* reconsider. Children's dictionaries are written for children, and are much better suited to their needs than adult dictionaries. Have you ever looked a word up in the dictionary and found that the definition of the word was the word itself? (*Belligerence* is the act of being *belligerent*? That's helpful.) Children's dictionaries, on the other hand, do a better job of defining words so that children can actually understand what they mean (belligerent means ready and eager to fight). The pictures next to the words are an added bonus.

Tutor Your Child to Reading Success does not require students or tutors to spend a lot of time looking up words in the dictionary, but you want one available for those times when your child comes across a word that he does not understand. Not to mention, you may not be familiar with all of the words in all of the lessons, and what a sterling example you will provide to your child when he sees you look up something in the dictionary! A few words have been chosen to teach a phonics concept (chromium, for example). These are not words we use in common, everyday speech, and learning the definition of these words will teach you and your child something new. How about that?

Cleared Refrigerator

Read it again, it says *cleared* refrigerator, not *cleaned* refrigerator! I don't care what is on the inside; I am asking that you devote a section of the outside of your refrigerator to displaying reading information. I have hung out with families that lived in tiny apartments and those that lived in huge mansions. One thing I know for sure, everybody hangs out in the kitchen! If you have children, it sometimes feels as though you *never* leave the kitchen! We stand in front of or walk past the fridge dozens of times each day. Papers and charts hanging there are less likely to be ignored or forgotten than those stuffed in the bottom of a drawer. Your child is more likely to review a list of words if they are staring him in the face. You will be more likely to suggest that he reads those words if you *see* them, as well.

My refrigerator is packed with pictures, papers, cards, magnets, clips and all sorts of stuff. Every few months I try to clear it off, but the space is soon gobbled up. Right now one side is completely covered with my son's sight word cards. He walks by, points to a word and reads, "The, to, girl, boy!" and keeps going. A little review never hurt anybody. There's no way I'm taking those cards down.

Access to a Copy Machine

The lessons, lists, flash cards, game boards and other materials in this book are your originals to copy. Some pages are for the tutor, some are for the student, and you will need to keep track of them all. We will be discussing this in depth, just understand that you will be making a fair amount of copies, especially in the beginning. It is worth your time to find an inexpensive (or free) copy machine to use. Lay-flat binding allows you to make good, straight copies and keep the book open to a particular page during tutoring sessions. Use removable tabs to flag pages that you need to copy so that you aren't running back and forth to the copier.

It is your book, and you can tear it apart if you choose, of course, but I recommend that you do not pull out any pages or mark them permanently. If you need to use a particular page, make a copy. If the copy becomes misplaced or damaged, you can easily go back to the book.

How This Book Is Organized

Countless hours were spent thinking about the best way to lay out <u>Tutor Your Child to Reading Success</u>. I sought the most natural and logical way to organize information so that busy parents could find what they needed quickly and easily. I remembered frantically searching through teacher's manuals looking for instructions that some publisher must have decided to hide as a cruel joke. The information I needed always seemed to be buried two hundred pages from where I needed it. I also thought about the times I sat in a class or seminar and wanted to scream at the professor, "What is the point? Just get to it!" With these thoughts in mind, I tried to design a straightforward and helpful book.

Like with Like

<u>Tutor Your Child to Reading Success</u> is organized into four main sections:
  -**Part 1**, chapters one through four, is an introduction to reading and tutoring.
  -**Part 2** includes chapters five through eight. In this section, parents learn how to give, score and interpret sight word, phonics and fluency assessments (tests). All assessments and materials

are easily found in the **Appendix Part 2 ASSESSMENTS** at the end of Part 2, not the end of the book.

-**Part 3** includes chapters nine through twelve. Here, parents learn how to teach sight word, phonics and fluency lessons based on what they learned from Part 2. **Appendix Part 3 LESSONS** makes quick work of locating lessons, games, materials and references.

-**Part 4** includes the **Afterword, Bibliography and Recommended Reading, Glossary and Definitions**, and **Index**.

Everything But the Kitchen Sink

Whether your child is in the 1st grade or 7th, you can use this book to tutor your child in reading. As a child's reading improves, they will be able to move to the next step without having to purchase additional volumes.

Assessments, lessons, games- it's all here! Of course, parents may choose to supplement the lessons in this book, but I have worked extremely hard so that they won't have to do so. I even show you how to use your child's own books to teach fluency lessons.

Easy to Find Directions

On the top, right-hand side of every assessment, parents will be told who the assessment is meant for, what it is meant to assess, and how to give the assessment properly. These directions take up precious space, but who wants to hunt around looking for instructions? How much nicer to have instructions literally at one's fingertips.

Minimum of Theory

Although I enjoy reading the latest reading research, I know that most parents don't have the time or the inclination to read page after page of sometimes dry and boring reading theory. Tutor Your Own Child to Reading Success is a practical and hands-on book for busy parents. Instead of too much theory, parents will find real information to use tutoring their children. My teaching methods and the lessons in this book are based on educational research and my experience as a teacher and tutor. If parents would like to read the theory behind the lessons, they will find pertinent books and articles listed in the **Bibliography and Recommended Reading** at the end of Part 4.

One last word about using this book: take your time! Don't feel rushed to cover every lesson this week, or even this month. Find a learning pace that matches your child's style and temperament. Learning should be fun and energizing, not stressful and exhausting. Review and repeat lessons until your child has mastered the concept or idea you are trying to teach. Teachers have so many students and so much material to cover. They must move on whether or not a child needs extra time. This is one of the most frustrating aspects about teaching. As a parent, you are in the position to give your child as much time as he needs. Enjoy it and consider yourself very lucky.

I cannot remember what I had for dinner last night, but I have clear and vivid memories of being six years old and reading with my mother. She put my baby sister down for a nap (the one *I* later taught to read!), came to my bedroom and spent time with me. I knew that my mother was busy and had other, very important "Mom things" to do, but there she was helping me with my reading. My mother didn't have to tell me that reading was important and that she loved me. Her actions made those things perfectly clear.

You are doing a wonderful thing.

PART TWO

DETERMINE WHAT THEY DON'T KNOW

CHAPTER 5

ASSESSMENTS

YOU HAVE TO KNOW WHERE YOU STAND BEFORE YOU TAKE YOUR FIRST STEP

Assessment is a fancy word for test, and I use them interchangeably. By any name, parents know all about tests. The testing starts before our children are born. Technicians, doctors, and nurses listen, prod and poke while we hold our breath, cross our fingers and pray for good news. Once our children actually enter this world, more tests follow. The Apgar Test, which is given just one minute after birth, evaluates a newborn's physical condition after delivery, and could be called a child's first report card.

To take the medical analogy further, if you were exhausted and went to the doctor, what is the very first thing she would do? Try to diagnose the problem, naturally. It only makes sense that before the doctor prescribes a course of treatment or medication, she would need to know what, exactly, was the matter. While this seems obvious, when it comes to children and reading, we often overlook the benefit of a diagnosis. Before we can figure out how to help a child become a good, strong, and excited reader, we need to pinpoint what they know and what they don't. Until we find the holes in the reading fabric, we can't begin to mend it.

Our educational system has been designed to rank and categorize our children, to give scores and assign grades. I am talking about testing with the *purpose to help those being tested.* Testing should give us the information we need to custom-tailor a tutoring plan that meets a child's needs and does not bore him silly. A little review never hurt anybody, but wasting precious time has hurt a whole lot of children.

In *Chapter 2 How Children Learn to Read* we talked about the Big Three- phonics, sight words and fluency. Parents must know where their children stand in *each* of those areas. What phonics lesson do they need? Which sight words are they missing? What are their fluency rates? This information comes from assessments. The doctor took some blood and ran a few tests.

She says, "The reason you are feeling so tired is because you are anemic. You have an iron deficiency. Here are some iron pills." I take the iron pills, I feel better. The basic idea is the same with reading assessment. If your son is having trouble with sight words, target your tutoring efforts to that area, and you will see immediate reading improvement.

Many parents are frustrated because they want to help, but have no idea where to start. Asking the teacher may or may not help as some teachers simply don't have specific information about what a student needs. *But what about all those tests my child takes*, you rightfully want to know. Standardized test results often come too late (the next school year) and may be too detailed to be of much use. I have been given standardized test results that ran pages long! In Tutor Your Child to Reading Success, parents will finally be able to get the diagnoses they need by administering simple tests that are easy to interpret.

STEPS AND GRADE LEVEL

From their very first day of school, children are put into groups and the labeling begins. I have actually heard teachers refer to learning groups in their class as "high" and "low"- in front of parents and students! I No wonder even the youngest students quickly decide that some kids are smart and some dumb. Overt or covert, intentional or unintentional, labeling persists throughout school, so you must do your best to avoid the practice at home. It is no accident that the assessments and lessons in this book are organized into *steps* and not grade levels. Steps bring to mind progress, going up, starting at the beginning and moving to higher ground.

> Step 1 Primary Grades 1-2
> Step 2 Middle Elementary Grades 3-4
> Step 3 Upper Elementary Grades 4-5+

Of course, parents need to know the level of a particular list of words, and that information is provided on tutor materials. There are no references to grade levels on student materials. I am not against progress; I am trying to avoid making children feel any worse about their reading abilities than they do already. Your 5th grader does not need to be reminded that he doesn't know

2nd grade sight words. He is reminded at school constantly that he is not reading at the 5th grade level. Children are smart and will probably figure out which steps correspond to which grade level, and for that reason some people believe that this is all a waste of time. "It's just semantics!" they say. Perhaps, but in <u>Tutor Your Child to Reading Success</u>, we intend for children to be excited about moving up, not disappointed about being behind.

TESTS AND ASSESSMENTS

Many of us have horrible memories of tests in school. Have you ever known a subject inside-out, had complete mastery, could explain it to someone else, but totally blanked out when you sat down for the test? How could you forget everything you knew so well only moments before? Naturally, you worried that the same thing would happen again, worked yourself into a state, and the exact same thing happened on the next test! You decided, "I don't do well on tests," and a pattern was born.

News flash- many children also have bad test memories, and their memories are fresher. They know what it is like to spend an hour Thursday evening studying spelling words, and then miss those same words on Friday's test. Parents, too, are perplexed by their children's spelling grades. "He KNEW those words, I'm telling you!" I believe you.

The idea of *anybody* giving your child a test makes him nervous. If this is the first time that Mom or Dad has *ever* done it, of course it's going to be totally weird. So, before we talk about how to give assessments, I want to stress a few things.

Be Honest

Children are a lot more astute than we give them credit for being. Be honest with your child about why you have decided to start tutoring. Use your own words, and be sincere. You might say, "Jesse, I've noticed that you have trouble reading your homework every night. I've been looking at some of your old report cards, and I think the problem might have started in second grade when you were sick and missed so much school. Whatever the reason, you need some help now. I know how smart you are, and it hurts me to see you struggle. Let's work on this together."

Please don't insult your child by sugarcoating the truth or not giving him any explanation about why you have decided to start tutoring.

Start Easy

You want your child to feel successful from the beginning, so always begin with assessments on which you know he will do well. Set the tone from the beginning that tutoring is going to be a fun, positive experience. This means that even if your son is in the 5th grade (Step 3), start with the Step 1 tests. These assessments will probably be very easy for him, but isn't it worth ten minutes to let your child feel *good* about his reading ability for a change?

Another reason that I recommend always beginning with Step 1 assessments is that it is deadly to make assumptions about what a child does and does not know. Your daughter may be in the 3rd grade, but that does not mean that she has mastered short vowel sounds.

I once made an awful mistake with one of my tutoring students. "My-Lai" was a 2nd grader. I inadvertently gave her a Step 2 (3rd and 4th grades) phonics test. The test was much too difficult, and almost from the beginning My-Lai was unable to read most of the words. Discouraged, she started mumbling and speaking in a low voice, which children often do when they are having trouble reading. Her body language- slumped shoulders, head down- was typical of someone that wanted to disappear. Halfway down the page, I realized that I had given her the wrong test!

I still want to kick myself. I did my best to repair the damage. "Oh my gosh! I gave you the wrong test! What was I thinking? This test is for fourth graders! I am so sorry! But, wait a minute! You knew some of those words! How did you do that?" I hope that I convinced her I was a fool and she the smart one.

Stay Positive

Don't pass up any opportunity to praise your child while tutoring. Your 6th grade son read a list of 3rd grade words. You may be thinking *thank goodness you know those words*! but you say, "You read all of those words! Time for something harder!" We are here to build a child's confidence and try to make up for all of the times during the school day that he feels badly because he isn't a good reader. Let's offset a huge deficit by putting deposits in the self-esteem bank whenever we can.

CHAPTER **6**

HOW TO GIVE SIGHT WORD ASSESSMENTS

Sight words, introduced in ***Chapter 2 How Children Learn to Read,*** are those words that children need to be able to read on sight and recognize instantly. Good readers do not sound out sight words or use context clues to read them. While sight words make up a sizable amount of what adults read (in the newspaper, for example), they are a *huge* part of children's reading, especially in the lower grades. Total knowledge and mastery of these words will make an amazing difference in your child's ability to not only read most of what he comes across, but to read it well and with understanding. For all of these reasons, I recommend that you begin testing sight words.

Begin testing all children with the Step 1 (Early 1st Grade) sight word test, regardless of grade level. We discussed why this is a good idea in the last chapter. Please note that there are *three* Step 1 sight word assessments: Early 1st Grade, Middle and Late 1st Grade, and Second Grade. This should give you an idea just how many sight words children are expected to learn in the lower grades. In fact, there aren't any Step 3 (5th grade and beyond) sight words. It is assumed that by then a child has learned all of the sight words in the English language! Remember to refer to the tests by steps, not grade level, when talking to your child.

Sight words lists are based on the *frequency* that words are found in grade level materials. So, the words from the Step 2 lists are the most common words found in 3rd and 4th grade books, but the words ought to be learned much earlier. It is for this reason that I recommend teaching all sight words in 1st and 2nd grades, or as soon as possible.

There are six sight word assessments. By the end of each grade, a student needs to know ALL of the sight words for that grade and all prior grades. 100 Most Common Sight Words and Colors, Number, Months and Days of the Week should be learned as soon as possible.

	1st Grade	*2nd Grade*	*3rd Grade*	*4th Grade & Beyond*
Step 1 **Early 1st Grade**	X	X	X	X
Step 1 **Mid-Late 1st Grade**	X	X	X	X
Step 1 **2nd Grade**	once 1st grd. Step 1 mastery is reached	X	X	X
Step 2 **3rd & 4th Grades**	once Step 1 mastery is reached	once Step 1 mastery is reached	X	X
100 Most Common	X	X	X	X
Colors, Numbers, Months, Days	X	X	X	X

Table 1 - Sight Word Testing

You don't want your son to feel badly for not knowing material that he shouldn't be expected to know! ***Fight the urge to just see if your child can complete a test that is at a higher grade level UNTIL he is breezing through the tests at his grade level.*** If your second grader received 100% on the Step 1 Early 1st Grade test, the Step 1 Middle and Late 1st Grade test *and* the Step 1- 2nd grade test, by all means give him the Step 2- 3rd and 4th Grades test. But, be careful.

> Preface it by saying, "It's amazing! You know all of the Step1 sight words! I have an idea! Do you want to see if you can read some of the Step 2 sight words? A lot of the words are pretty advanced. I'll only let you take the test if you promise not to get upset if it's too hard..."

Once your child has taken the appropriate assessments, you may choose to give them the 100 Most Common Sight Words and the Colors, Numbers, Months, and Days of the Week tests. Another alternative is to give these tests *after* your child has learned the sight words for their grade level.

In teacher training school, I was taught how to present lessons using a highly structured lesson plan format. Student teachers are told that this format is standard; that is, all teachers use it. Once I started actually teaching I found out the truth: most teachers modify the lesson plan format or discard it completely. The standard format isn't standard, after all! Because I believe that parents are on a race against time to help their children become masterful readers, <u>Tutor Your Child to Reading Success,</u> presents lessons using the pre-race rally, "Ready, on your marks, get set, go!"

1. Ready: MAKE COPIES

Turn to the **Appendix Part 2 ASSESSMENTS** and find the sight word assessments to **copy**. Save time and copy all of the assessments you expect to use in the foreseeable future, including 100 Most Common Sight Words and Colors, Numbers, Months, and Days of the Week. Each assessment is made up of two parts- the Tutor Copy, which is what you will be looking at, and the Student Copy, which is for your child. Remember to copy both sets. **Staple** each test separately to avoid dealing with loose pages everywhere. Put each test in a page protector and **store** in your binder.

When giving an assessment, I usually sit on the left and place the student on the right. Do what feels most comfortable to you. I recommend sitting at a desk or table so that you won't have to balance materials on your lap. You will also be able to write more easily. Once you have finished this testing phase and moved into teaching lessons and playing games, by all means sit on a couch or the floor!

2. On Your Marks: START TALKING

Set the tone from the beginning that, unlike school, testing with you is a relaxed affair. Give your child permission to make mistakes. Tell him that some of the sight words are easy, some are hard, and it is okay if he doesn't know them all.

Explain that you will be taking notes while he is reading his list of sight words. Get in the habit of writing and doodling on your paper periodically-even when your child has not made a mistake. Some children freeze up or lose their concentration every time they see you writing. You don't want them to think that the only time you write on the page is when they make a mistake. Eventually, they will ignore your writing all together, which will be especially helpful when doing fluency tests.

Say, "Here are some words called sight words. They call them sight words because these aren't the kind of words you sound out. These word you see and read. I expect that some of these sight words will be *easy* for you, some might be hard, but that's what I want to find out! Don't worry if you don't know all of them, ok? Here is your list of sight words (give him the Student Copy). I have a copy of the list, too (motion to your list). While you are reading your copy, I will write things down on my copy to remind me of things to talk about later. Don't worry about what I'm doing! Just do your best, ok?"

3. Get Set- MODEL TRACKING

Some children are easily distracted and have difficulty keeping their place while reading a long list of words. Show them how to keep their index finger under one word at time. After they have read the word, they can move their finger down the list to the next word. This is called tracking, and it is a good skill to have, especially when reading a paragraph or story.

If your son still has trouble staying on the word, use a 3 X 5 card or a folded piece of paper to cover the words below the one he is reading.

4. Go! START THE TEST

Basically, your child reads the list of words while you keep track of those words that he misreads on the Tutor Copy. Looking at your own page while your son reads another page might feel strange at first, but you will soon get used to it. Believe it or not, your kindergarten teacher wasn't born with the ability to read upside down; it took practice!

When your child comes to a word that he does not recognize, give him 3 or 4 seconds to figure it out, circle or highlight the word on your list in the 2nd Try column, and ask him to go to the next word. It is important to give him *wait time* of a few seconds, but no more. Do not give him the word or discuss his mistake. This is not instruction time; assessments are fact-finding missions. You will have plenty of time to teach him *every* sight word he misses.

If your child takes four or more seconds to read a sight word- even correctly- make a note of it next to the word on your copy. You may want to have this information later when teaching sight words.

Sometimes your child will read a word incorrectly (*the* for *they*). Circle or highlight the word on your list and write down what he does say. You might find that he misreads the same type of words or combinations. One must have enough information to spot a pattern.

When your son has completed the assessment, tell him that he did a good job. This is true whether or not he knew most of the sight words- he finished the test, didn't he? Never pass up an opportunity to praise your child. Concentrate on those sight words he did know and say, "My goodness! You knew so many of those sight words! Just think how much fun reading will be when you know ALL of them!"

Count the number of missed words and write that number on the Score line in the 1st Try column under the date. For example, if your son missed three words, write -3. Now you know exactly which sight words your son needs to learn- and you need to teach! After a few sight word lessons, give the test again. Next time, you will use the 2nd Try column and be able to quickly compare scores and marvel at your son's progress. Save this assessment in your binder.

Decide if you want to stop there or continue with another assessment. Don't be overzealous and over-test your child. For your first session, two tests are great. Go have a hot chocolate or take a walk around the park. Remember, you want your son to associate tutoring with good things, and being drilled and tested too much is not going to accomplish that.

Depending on your child's grade, it might take a week or two to complete all of the sight word assessments. Consider it time well-spent.

CHAPTER 7

HOW TO GIVE PHONICS ASSESSMENTS

Once you have completed the sight word assessments, it is time to move onto the phonics assessments. By this point, you and your child will probably feel like testing pros, and the phonics assessments will be a piece of cake!

 1. Ready: MAKE COPIES

You will find the phonics assessment in **Appendix Part 2 ASSESS-MENTS**. Once again, start at the beginning, Phonics Test Step 1. See Table 2 to determine when to stop testing. Reminder: the grade level information is for the tutor, not the student. When referring to the assessments, always call them steps.

	1st Grade	*2nd Grade*	*3rd Grade*	*4th Grade*	*5th Grade & Beyond*
Step 1	X	X	X	X	X
Step 2			X	X	X
Step 3					X

Table 2 - Stop testing when you reach your child's current grade level. You don't want your daughter feeling bad for not knowing material she shouldn't be expected to know.

2. On Your Marks: START TALKING

Once again, you want to tell your child what is about to happen and put her at ease.

Say, "We've been working hard figuring our which sight words you know. You know a lot! Now it's time to look at some other words. If you need to, it's okay to sound out these words. Some of them are going to be pretty easy and some are really hard. Don't worry about it. Just relax and do your best."

3. Get Set: MODEL TRACKING

Remind your child to isolate each word by using her finger or a piece of folded paper.

4. Go! START THE TEST

Phonics and sight word tests are similar in that for both tests students read words and tutors keep track of which words students are unable to read. The major difference between the tests is that with sight word assessments, students read only one column of words; in phonics assessments, students may have to read from other columns of words.

Have your child read the words on her test. This will correspond to the first column of words on your tutor copy. Circle or mark any misread words. When your child has read all of the words, find *any missed words and have your child read the words in the columns next to the missed one*. These words, in the columns headed 2ⁿᵈ Check, 3ʳᵈ Check, and so on, follow the same phonics rule as the first missed word, found on the Student Test. For example, on Phonics Test Step 1, the 14ᵗʰ test word is *rain*. If your child misreads this word, wait until the end of the test, find the word on your tutor copy and say, "This row has some words similar to *rain*. Can you read any of these?" You need to find out if your child knows the digraph *ai* and just made a mistake with *rain-* or if she really does not know how to read *ai*. Whether or not she is able to read *tail, bait, maid* and *claim* will give you that information. Wait until she has read all the words before you mark or circle any that she misses. It is important to do this type of checking with *every* word your child misses on a phonics assessment. Sometimes a child will misread a word (*ran* instead of *rain*), but know the phonics some place else. You don't want to spend days teaching a phonics lesson that your daughter doesn't need!

It has often happened that while testing for one phonics rule, I find that a whole other phonics lesson needs to be taught! This is due to the fact that so many words contain more than one phonics rule. The word *rescue* contains a short vowel, a hard c, and a long u. (Don't worry if you don't know what those mean!) You need to know which phonics are causing a problem. The best way to acquire that information is to not only mark that a word has been misread, but write down exactly what was said.

I once tutored a 5ᵗʰ grade girl that was confused by short and long vowel sounds (the difference between *cap* and *cape*, for example). This is the kind of thing that should be taught and mastered in the early grades- 1ˢᵗ and 2ⁿᵈ. Imagine how difficult reading was for this 5ᵗʰ grader! Honestly, I was impressed by how many other phonics rules she did know- blends, silent letters, etc. By writing down exactly how she pronounced each word, I figured out the problem, and we worked on long and short vowel sounds. If I had simply put a big, fat check next to *every* missed word and not written anything down, I would have thought that she knew next to nothing! And, boy, would I have been wrong!

This brings me to my next point: if your child does have a lot of difficulty on a particular test, keep in mind that when you ask her to read the words from the other columns, there will be a lot of correction marks staring her in the face. Do you remember how *you* felt when your teacher returned *your* test covered with red marks and Xs? Consider using a pencil or a light pen when marking phonics assessments or cover the first column of words when your child looks at your copy or check the **correct** words and write notes next to the misread ones.

Why not have separate lists for each phonics rule instead of asking stu-

#							
36	bang	ding	anything	bong	song	lung	36 -ng
37	(knack)	(knee)	knew	(knit)	knock	(knot)	37- kn
38	(comb)	(tomb)	(crumb)				38 -mb
39	catch	match	itch	ditch	pitch	hutch	39 -tch
40	badge	pledge	lodge	budge	bridge		40 -dge
41	(cage)	(giant)	(bridge)	(danger)	(gentle)		41- soft g
42	ice	nice	face	cent	circle	center	42- soft c
43							43- ail

Table 3 - Phonics assessment example

dents to read the tutor copy? Keeping track of hundred of phonics lists, recording which words were missed, transferring that information onto the tutor copy…talk about an organizational nightmare! This is much *easier*, believe me.

As a general rule, if a student misses two or more words from a row, I know that I need to teach that phonics lesson. I will start with those lessons that have the most words marked as missed. Take a look at the test on the previous page.

It is clear that I should begin teaching *soft g, kn* and *mb*. Relax, you will learn how to teach phonics lessons in **Chapter 11 How to Teach Phonics Lessons!** At this point, all you need to do is date the phonics assessments and put them neatly in your tutoring binder.

Next stop- fluency assessments!

CHAPTER 8

HOW TO GIVE FLUENCY ASSESSMENTS

Just when you thought you had it made, it's time to learn something new. Fluency assessments are a bit different than sight word and phonics assessments, but the goal is the same- find out what your child does and does not know. Fluency is a hot topic these days, and many children are used to taking fluency tests in school. Some might even know their CWPM (correct words per minute) score. That's the good news.

The not-so-good news is that the preoccupation with results and higher scores has caused some teachers to lose sight of the fact that the point of increasing fluency is so that children can comprehend, or understand, what they read. Unfortunately, many children have been encouraged- directly and indirectly- to go for speed. They are told to read as fast as they can. Actual comprehension is irrelevant. So, we have students playing a game, racing against the teacher's timer, and nobody is worried whether or not they understand a word. Ugh.

An entire subculture exists around scoring fluency assessments. There are all kinds of signs, symbols, proofreading marks, and special shorthand one can memorize and use. Many teachers and reading specialists make notes on their students' fluency tests that look like hieroglyphics! If they understand their special language and use it to help students- fantastic. Personally, I have found that the simpler my notes, the more likely I am to remember what they mean!

If your child (student) does this...	*You (parent) do this...*
Reads a word incorrectly	Circle the word and write down what they actually said above it
Skips a word	Cross it out
Skips an entire line	Cross out the line
Substitutes a word that changes meaning (dog for house)	Insert a /\ and write down what they said
Substitutes a word that does NOT change meaning (glass for cup)	Do nothing. I don't count this as wrong

This is my system, and it works for me. Of course, you are welcome to create your style of marking fluency assessments. Just don't get too fancy- you want to be able to look at that fluency test six months from now and understand what happened. If your marks clearly show you how many words your son read, which words he misread, which words he skipped, and where he inserted words- your system is fine.

I strove to create fluency tests that would do more than simply tell parents how fast a child reads, but also tell them which *types* of words that child needs to learn. This is why the tutor copy fluency assessments in <u>Tutor Your Child to Reading Success</u> look different than typical fluency assessments. Below many words will be a code that describes it. For example, under the word *every*, you will find 'S2' indicating that the word is from the 2nd Grade sight word (S2) list; *ai* is found under *rain*. Along with the sight word and phonics assessments, this information can help you focus your tutoring sessions.

 Unlike sight word and phonics assessments, fluency assessments are timed. You will need a reliable watch with a secondhand, or a timer. I have issues with watches. I always look away during the test, forget when I started, and have to ask students to start over! I use timers; kids are fascinated by them. If you choose to use one, don't make a big deal out of it or your child will drive you crazy. Show your son the new timer, let him see how it works, allow him a few minutes to play with it- then treat it like any other boring office tool. I always put the shiny, distracting timer on my left, as far away from my student as possible. Also, if you are going to be testing in a public and/ or quiet place, like a café or a library, don't use your wake-the-dead kitchen timer! Silence it immediately when it beeps.

Fluency assessments can be stressful. Children want to read fast, and adults want to jump in and blurt out a word before a poor child has the chance to figure it out. As soon as a child pauses, our first inclination is to say the word for them. This is a natural, but hardly helpful, tendency. Waiting a few moments and gently providing the word is called *prompting*. More than a few articles have been written on this subject, but the three things to keep in mind when giving a fluency test or listening to a child read are: patience, patience, patience. Allow your child three seconds (1, 1000, 2, 2000, 3, 3000) to figure out a word. Both of you will be amazed at how many times he does just that! If, after three long seconds, he is still unable to read the word, say, "Keep going." If he skips a word or line, don't say anything at all. Your job is to keep track of what he *is* reading. Remember, this is a fact-finding mission. You want to find out how fast and how well he reads. You will have plenty of time to improve that fluency score, teacher!

1. Get Ready- MAKE COPIES

Find the fluency assessments in the **Appendix Part 2 ASSESSMENTS**. You know the drill- start with the first assessment, regardless of your child's age and grade level. Psychologically, it is better for your son to laughingly breeze through his first fluency assessment than to struggle from the gate. Use the chart below to determine how many tests to copy.

Table 4 – Fluency Testing

	1st Grade	2nd Grade	3rd Grade	4th Grade	5th Grade	6th Grade & Beyond
Step 1 Early 1st Grade	X	X	X	X	X	X
Step 1 Mid 1st Grade	X	X	X	X	X	X
Step 1 Late 1st Grade	X	X	X	X	X	X
Step 1 2nd Grade		X	X	X	X	X
Step 2 3rd Grade			X	X	X	X
Step 2 4th Grade				X	X	X
Step 3 5th Grade					X	X
Step 3 6th Grade						X

2. On Your Mark- START TALKING

Say, "Good news! No more long lists of words! Now you get to read some real sentences! These are short little paragraphs, but I want you to read them carefully. When you are finished, you should be able to tell me what you've read. If you come to a word that you don't know, try to figure it out, but don't spend too much time on it. It's okay to skip a word that you don't know. I am going to be writing stuff down like I did before, so don't pay attention to me, okay? Ready?"

3. Get Set- TRACKING

Remind your child to use their index finger as a tracker to keep place while they read. This is especially important when reading sentences and paragraphs.

Set your timer for 1 minute.

4. Go! START THE TEST

Say, "Start reading when you're ready."

Wait until your child reads the first word to start the timer. You will write on your tutor copy while your child reads from their student copy. Do NOT correct your child's reading. When the timer goes off, make a long line (or any distinguishing mark) after the last word your child reads. Count the number of words read (WPM), and subtract the number of missed (skipped or incorrect) words. You now have your son's CWPM (correct words per minute) score. Write this number and the date on your Tutor Copy.

Ask your child to summarize the paragraph in his own words. Did he understand it? If you ask him a simple question, "Who was the story about?" can he answer it? There is no point in reading without comprehension.

Be sure to wait until you and your son have been tutoring for some time before you retest with the same fluency assessments. If you son sees the same tests often enough, he will begin to memorize them! Memorization has its place, but not when measuring fluency. You want to know whether or not your child can actually read the sight words and phonics you have taught them. How will you know if he has really learned how to read the word *scene-* or if he just remembers the assessment?

The next time you give this assessment, you will see how much faster your child is reading, which words in particular he has learned and which kinds of mistakes he no longer makes.

APPENDIX PART *2*
ASSESSMENTS

CONTENTS

Tutor Copy
1. Copy this page & keep in binder
2. Mark missed words as student reads from student copy
3. Note date & score
4. Use sight word lesson plans to teach missed words
5. Retest until mastery is reached

Sight Words- 100 Most Common
(S100)

	1st Try Date_____ Score_____	2nd Try Date_____ Score_____	3rd Try Date_____ Score_____	4th Try Date_____ Score_____	5th Try Date_____ Score_____
1	the	the	the	the	the
2	of	of	of	of	of
3	and	and	and	and	and
4	a	a	a	a	a
5	to	to	to	to	to
6	in	in	in	in	in
7	is	is	is	is	is
8	you	you	you	you	you
9	that	that	that	that	that
10	it	it	it	it	it
11	he	he	he	he	he
12	for	for	for	for	for

(S100)

13	was	was	was	was	was
14	on	on	on	on	on
15	are	are	are	are	are
16	as	as	as	as	as
17	with	with	with	with	with
18	his	his	his	his	his
19	they	they	they	they	they
20	at	at	at	at	at
21	be	be	be	be	be
22	this	this	this	this	this
23	from	from	from	from	from
24	I	I	I	I	I
25	have	have	have	have	have
26	or	or	or	or	or
27	by	by	by	by	by
28	one	one	one	one	one
29	had	had	had	had	had
30	not	not	not	not	not

(S100)

31	but	but	but	but	but
32	what	what	what	what	what
33	all	all	all	all	all
34	were	were	were	were	were
35	when	when	when	when	when
36	we	we	we	we	we
37	there	there	there	there	there
38	can	can	can	can	can
39	an	an	an	an	an
40	your	your	your	your	your
41	which	which	which	which	which
42	their	their	their	their	their
43	said	said	said	said	said
44	if	if	if	if	if
45	do	do	do	do	do
46	will	will	will	will	will
47	each	each	each	each	each
48	about	about	about	about	about

(S100)

49	how	how	how	how	how
50	up	up	up	up	up
51	out	out	out	out	out
52	them	them	them	them	them
53	then	then	then	then	then
54	she	she	she	she	she
55	many	many	many	many	many
56	some	some	some	some	some
57	so	so	so	so	so
58	these	these	these	these	these
59	would	would	would	would	would
60	other	other	other	other	other
61	into	into	into	into	into
62	has	has	has	has	has
63	more	more	more	more	more
64	her	her	her	her	her
65	two	two	two	two	two
66	like	like	like	like	like

(S100)

67	him	him	him	him	him
68	see	see	see	see	see
69	time	time	time	time	time
70	could	could	could	could	could
71	no	no	no	no	no
72	make	make	make	make	make
73	than	than	than	than	than
74	first	first	first	first	first
75	been	been	been	been	been
76	its	its	its	its	its
77	who	who	who	who	who
78	now	now	now	now	now
79	people	people	people	people	people
80	my	my	my	my	my
81	made	made	made	made	made
82	over	over	over	over	over
83	did	did	did	did	did
84	down	down	down	down	down

(S100)

85	only	only	only	only	only
86	way	way	way	way	way
87	find	find	find	find	find
88	use	use	use	use	use
89	may	may	may	may	may
90	water	water	water	water	water
91	long	long	long	long	long
92	little	little	little	little	little
93	very	very	very	very	very
94	after	after	after	after	after
95	words	words	words	words	words
96	called	called	called	called	called
97	just	just	just	just	just
98	where	where	where	where	where
99	most	most	most	most	most
100	know	know	know	know	know

Student Test
1. Copy this test
2. Flag or protect to use again
3. Date & score tutor copy

Sight Words (S100)

1	the
2	of
3	and
4	a
5	to
6	in
7	is
8	you
9	that
10	it
11	he
12	for

(S100)

13	was
14	on
15	are
16	as
17	with
18	his
19	they
20	at
21	be
22	this
23	from
24	I
25	have
26	or
27	by
28	one
29	had
30	not

(S100)

31	but
32	what
33	all
34	were
35	when
36	we
37	there
38	can
39	an
40	your
41	which
42	their
43	said
44	if
45	do
46	will
47	each
48	about

(S100)

49	how
50	up
51	out
52	them
53	then
54	she
55	many
56	some
57	so
58	these
59	would
60	other
61	into
62	has
63	more
64	her
65	two
66	like

(S100)

67	him
68	see
69	time
70	could
71	no
72	make
73	than
74	first
75	been
76	its
77	who
78	now
79	people
80	my
81	made
82	over
83	did
84	down

(S100)

85	only
86	way
87	find
88	use
89	may
90	water
91	long
92	little
93	very
94	after
95	words
96	called
97	just
98	where
99	most
100	know

Tutor Copy
1. Copy this page & keep in binder
2. Mark missed words as student reads from student copy
3. Note date & score
4. Use sight word lesson plans to teach missed words
5. Retest until mastery is reached

Sight Words- Step 1 (Early 1st Grade) (SE1)

	1st Try Date_____ Score_____	2nd Try Date_____ Score_____	3rd Try Date_____ Score_____	4th Try Date_____ Score_____	5th Try Date_____ Score_____
1	would	would	would	would	would
2	make	make	make	make	make
3	like	like	like	like	like
4	him	him	him	him	him
5	into	into	into	into	into
6	time	time	time	time	time
7	has	has	has	has	Has
8	look	look	look	look	look
9	more	more	more	more	more
10	write	write	write	write	write
11	other	other	other	other	other
12	about	about	about	about	about

(SE1)

13	out	out	out	out	out
14	many	many	many	many	many
15	then	then	then	then	then
16	them	them	them	them	them
17	these	these	these	these	these
18	so	so	so	so	so
19	some	some	some	some	some
20	her	her	her	her	her
21	use	use	use	use	use
22	an	an	an	an	an
23	each	each	each	each	each
24	which	which	which	which	which
25	do	do	do	do	do
26	how	how	how	how	how
27	their	their	their	their	their
28	If	if	if	if	if
29	will	will	will	will	will
30	up	up	up	up	up

(SE1)

31	not	not	not	not	not
32	what	what	what	what	what
33	all	all	all	all	all
34	were	were	were	were	were
35	we	we	we	we	we
36	when	when	when	when	when
37	your	your	your	your	your
38	can	can	can	can	can
39	said	said	said	said	said
40	there	there	there	there	there
41	be	be	be	be	be
42	this	this	this	this	this
43	have	have	have	have	have
44	from	from	from	from	from
45	or	or	or	or	or
46	one	one	one	one	one
47	had	had	had	had	had
48	by	by	by	by	by

(SE1)

49	word	word	word	word	word
50	but	but	but	but	but
51	he	he	he	he	he
52	was	was	was	was	was
53	for	for	for	for	for
54	on	on	on	on	on
55	are	are	are	are	are
56	as	as	as	as	as
57	with	with	with	with	with
58	his	his	his	his	his
59	they	they	they	they	they
60	I	I	I	I	I
61	the	the	the	the	the
62	of	of	of	of	of
63	and	and	and	and	and
64	a	a	a	a	a
65	To	to	to	to	to
66	in	in	in	in	in

(SE1)

67	Is	is	is	is	is
68	you	you	you	you	you
69	that	that	that	that	that
70	It	it	it	it	it

Student Test
1. Copy this test
2. Flag or protect to use again
3. Date & score tutor copy

Sight Words- (SE1)

1	would
2	make
3	like
4	him
5	into
6	time
7	has
8	look
9	more
10	write
11	other
12	about

(SE1)

13	out
14	many
15	then
16	them
17	these
18	so
19	some
20	her
21	use
22	an
23	each
24	which
25	do
26	how
27	their
28	if
29	will
30	up

(SE1)

31	not
32	what
33	all
34	were
35	we
36	when
37	your
38	can
39	said
40	there
41	be
42	this
43	have
44	from
45	or
46	one
47	had
48	by

(SE1)

49	word
50	but
51	he
52	was
53	for
54	on
55	are
56	as
57	with
58	his
59	they
60	I
61	the
62	of
63	and
64	a
65	to
66	in

(SE1)

67	is
68	you
69	that
70	it

Tutor Copy
1. Copy this page & keep in binder
2. Mark missed words as student reads from student copy
3. Note date & score
4. Use sight word lesson plans to teach missed words
5. Retest until mastery is reached

Sight Words- Step 1 (Middle & Late 1st Grade) (SML1)

	1st TryDate_____ Score_____	2nd TryDate_____ Score_____	3rd TryDate_____ Score_____	4th TryDate_____ Score_____	5th TryDate_____ Score_____
1.	go	go	go	go	go
2	see	see	see	see	see
3	number	number	number	number	number
4	no	no	no	no	no
5	way	way	way	way	way
6	could	could	could	could	could
7	people	people	people	people	people
8	my	my	my	my	my
9	than	than	than	than	than
10	first	first	first	first	first
11	most	most	most	most	most
12	very	very	very	very	very

(SML1)

13	after	after	after	after	after
14	thing	thing	thing	thing	thing
15	our	our	our	our	our
16	just	just	just	just	just
17	name	name	name	name	name
18	sentence	sentence	sentence	sentence	sentence
19	good	good	good	good	good
20	man	man	man	man	man
21	only	only	only	only	only
22	little	little	little	little	little
23	work	work	work	work	work
24	know	know	know	know	know
25	place	place	place	place	place
26	year	year	year	year	year
27	live	live	live	live	live
28	me	me	me	me	me
29	back	back	back	back	back
30	give	give	give	give	give

(SML1)

31	day	day	day	day	day
32	did	did	did	did	did
33	get	get	get	get	get
34	made	made	made	made	made
35	may	may	may	may	may
36	part	part	part	part	part
37	over	over	over	over	over
38	new	new	new	new	new
39	sound	sound	sound	sound	sound
40	take	take	take	take	take
41	water	water	water	water	water
42	been	been	been	been	been
43	call	call	call	call	call
44	who	who	who	who	who
45	oil	oil	oil	oil	oil
46	its	its	its	its	its
47	now	now	now	now	now
48	find	find	find	find	find

(SML1)

49	long	long	long	long	long
50	down	down	down	down	down
51	off	off	off	off	off
52	again	again	again	again	again
53	land	land	land	land	land
54	men	men	men	men	men
55	went	went	went	went	went
56	spell	spell	spell	spell	spell
57	need	need	need	need	need
58	ask	ask	ask	ask	ask
59	kind	kind	kind	kind	kind
60	picture	picture	picture	picture	picture
61	home	home	home	home	home
62	more	more	more	more	more
63	why	why	why	why	why
64	different	different	different	different	different
65	try	try	try	try	try
66	read	read	read	read	read

(SML1)

67	show	show	show	show	show
68	such	such	such	such	such
69	also	also	also	also	also
70	form	form	form	form	form
71	around	around	around	around	around
72	well	well	well	well	well
73	want	want	want	want	want
74	end	end	end	end	end
75	set	set	set	set	set
76	large	large	large	large	large
77	even	even	even	even	even
78	small	small	small	small	small
79	turn	turn	turn	turn	turn
80	another	another	another	another	another
81	put	put	put	put	put
82	three	three	three	three	three
83	must	must	must	must	must
84	even	even	even	even	even

(SML1)

85	because	because	because	because	because
86	big	big	big	big	big
87	before	before	before	before	before
88	follow	follow	follow	follow	follow
89	too	too	too	too	too
90	boy	boy	boy	boy	boy
91	old	old	old	old	old
92	great	great	great	great	great
93	same	same	same	same	same
94	where	where	where	where	where
95	any	any	any	any	any
96	came	came	came	came	came
97	line	line	line	line	line
99	tell	tell	tell	tell	tell
100	think	think	think	think	think
101	much	much	much	much	much
102	man	man	man	man	man
103	through	through	through	through	through

(SML1)

104	mean	mean	mean	mean	mean
105	right	right	right	right	right
106	say	say	say	say	say
107	help	help	help	help	help

Student Test
1. Copy this test
2. Flag or protect to use again
3. Date & score tutor copy

Sight Words- (SML1)

1	go
2	see
3	number
4	no
5	way
6	could
7	people
8	my
9	than
10	first
11	most
12	very

(SML1)

13	after
14	thing
15	our
16	just
17	name
18	sentence
19	good
20	man
21	only
22	little
23	work
24	know
25	place
26	year
27	live
28	me
29	back
30	give

(SML1)

31	day
32	did
33	get
34	made
35	may
36	part
37	over
38	new
39	sound
40	take
41	water
42	been
43	call
44	who
45	oil
46	its
47	now
48	find

(SML1)

49	long
50	down
51	off
52	again
53	land
54	men
55	went
56	spell
57	need
58	ask
59	kind
60	picture
61	home
62	more
63	why
64	different
65	try
66	read

(SML1)

67	show
68	such
69	also
70	form
71	around
72	well
73	want
74	end
75	set
76	large
77	even
78	small
79	turn
80	another
81	put
82	three
83	must
84	even

(SML1)

85	because
86	big
87	before
88	follow
89	too
90	boy
91	old
92	great
93	same
94	where
95	any
96	came
97	line
99	tell
100	think
101	much
102	man
103	through

(SML1)

104	mean
105	right
106	say
107	help

Tutor Copy
1. Copy this page & keep in binder
2. Mark missed words as student reads from student copy
3. Note date & score
4. Use sight word lesson plans to teach missed words
5. Retest until mastery is reached

Sight Words- Step 1 (2nd Grade)
(S2)

	1st Try Date_____ Score_____	2nd Try Date_____ Score_____	3rd Try Date_____ Score_____	4th Try Date_____ Score_____	5th Try Date_____ Score_____
1	study	study	study	study	study
2	still	still	still	still	still
3	learn	learn	learn	learn	learn
4	should	should	should	should	should
5	America	America	America	America	America
6	world	world	world	world	world
7	high	high	high	high	high
8	every	every	every	every	every
9	near	near	near	near	near
10	add	add	add	add	add
11	air	air	air	air	air
12	away	away	away	away	away

(S2)

13	animal	animal	animal	animal	animal
14	house	house	house	house	house
15	point	point	point	point	point
16	page	page	page	page	page
17	letter	letter	letter	letter	letter
18	mother	mother	mother	mother	mother
19	answer	answer	answer	answer	answer
20	found	found	found	found	found
21	move	move	move	move	move
22	try	try	try	try	try
23	kind	kind	kind	kind	kind
24	hand	hand	hand	hand	hand
25	picture	picture	picture	picture	picture
26	again	again	again	again	again
27	change	change	change	change	change
28	off	off	off	off	off
29	play	play	play	play	play
30	spell	spell	spell	spell	spell

Student Test
1. Copy this test
2. Flag or protect to use again
3. Date & score tutor copy

Sight Words- (S2)

1	study
2	still
3	learn
4	should
5	America
6	world
7	high
8	every
9	near
10	add
11	air
12	away

(S2)

13	animal
14	house
15	point
16	page
17	letter
18	mother
19	answer
20	found
21	move
22	try
23	kind
24	hand
25	picture
26	again
27	change
28	off
29	play
30	spell

Tutor Copy
1. Copy this page & keep in working binder
2. Mark missed words as student reads from student copy
3. Note date & score
4. Use sight word lesson plans to teach missed words
5. Retest until mastery is reached

Sight Words- Step 2 (3rd and 4th Grades) (S34)

	1st Try Date_____ Score_____	2nd Try Date_____ Score_____	3rd Try Date_____ Score_____	4th Try Date_____ Score_____	5th Try Date_____ Score_____
1	tree	tree	tree	tree	tree
2	never	never	never	never	never
3	start	start	start	start	start
4	city	city	city	city	city
5	earth	earth	earth	earth	earth
6	eye	eye	eye	eye	eye
7	light	light	light	light	light
8	thought	thought	thought	thought	thought
9	head	head	head	head	head
10	under	under	under	under	under
11	story	story	story	story	story
12	saw	saw	saw	saw	saw

(S34)

13	left	left	left	left	left
14	don't	don't	don't	don't	don't
15	few	few	few	few	few
16	while	while	while	while	while
17	along	along	along	along	along
18	might	might	might	might	might
19	chose	chose	chose	chose	chose
20	something	something	something	something	something
21	seem	seem	seem	seem	seem
22	next	next	next	next	next
23	hard	hard	hard	hard	hard
24	open	open	open	open	open
25	example	example	example	example	example
26	begin	begin	begin	begin	begin
27	life	life	life	life	life
28	always	always	always	always	always
29	those	those	those	those	those
30	both	both	both	both	both

(S34)

31	paper	paper	paper	paper	paper
32	together	together	together	together	together
33	got	got	got	got	got
34	group	group	group	group	group
35	often	often	often	often	often
36	run	run	run	run	run
37	important	important	important	important	important
38	until	until	until	until	until
39	children	children	children	children	children
40	side	side	side	side	side
41	feet	feet	feet	feet	feet
42	car	car	car	car	car
43	mile	mile	mile	mile	mile
44	night	night	night	night	night
45	walk	walk	walk	walk	walk
46	white	white	white	white	white
47	sea	sea	sea	sea	sea
48	began	began	began	began	began

(S34)

49	grow	grow	grow	grow	grow
50	took	took	took	took	took
51	river	river	river	river	river
52	four	four	four	four	four
53	carry	carry	carry	carry	carry
54	state	state	state	state	state
55	once	once	once	once	once
56	book	book	book	book	book
57	hear	hear	hear	hear	hear
58	stop	stop	stop	stop	stop
59	without	without	without	without	without
60	second	second	second	second	second
61	almost	almost	almost	almost	almost
62	let	let	let	let	let
63	above	above	above	above	above
64	girl	girl	girl	girl	girl
65	sometimes	sometimes	sometimes	sometimes	sometimes
66	mountain	mountain	mountain	mountain	mountain

(S34)

67	cut	cut	cut	cut	cut
68	young	young	young	young	young
69	talk	talk	talk	talk	talk
70	soon	soon	soon	soon	soon
71	late	late	late	late	late
72	miss	miss	miss	miss	miss
73	idea	idea	idea	idea	Idea
74	enough	enough	enough	enough	enough
75	eat	eat	eat	eat	eat
76	face	face	face	face	face
77	watch	watch	watch	watch	watch
78	far	far	far	far	far
79	Indian	Indian	Indian	Indian	Indian
80	really	really	really	really	really
81	list	list	list	list	list
82	song	song	song	song	song
83	being	being	being	being	being
84	leave	leave	leave	leave	leave

(S34)

85	family	family	family	family	family
86	its	its	its	its	its

Student Test
1. Copy this test
2. Flag or protect to use again
3. Date & score tutor copy

Sight Words (S34)

1	tree
2	never
3	start
4	city
5	earth
6	eye
7	light
8	thought
9	head
10	under
11	story
12	saw

(S34)

13	left
14	don't
15	few
16	while
17	along
18	might
19	chose
20	something
21	seem
22	next
23	hard
24	open
25	example
26	begin
27	life
28	always
29	those
30	both

(S34)

31	paper
32	together
33	got
34	group
35	often
36	run
37	important
38	until
39	children
40	side
41	feet
42	car
43	mile
44	night
45	walk
46	white
47	sea
48	began

(S34)

49	grow
50	took
51	river
52	four
53	carry
54	state
55	once
56	book
57	hear
58	stop
59	without
60	second
61	almost
62	let
63	above
64	girl
65	sometimes
66	mountain

(S34)

67	cut
68	young
69	talk
70	soon
71	late
72	miss
73	idea
74	enough
75	eat
76	face
77	watch
78	far
79	Indian
80	really
81	list
82	song
83	being
84	leave
85	family
86	its

Tutor Copy
1. Copy this page & keep in binder
2. Mark missed words as student reads from student copy
3. Note date & score
4. Use sight word lesson plans to teach missed words

5. Retest until mastery is reached

Sight Words-
Colors, Numbers, Months, Days of the Week
(S)

	1st Try Date_____ Score_____	2nd Try Date_____ Score_____	3rd Try Date_____ Score_____	4th Try Date_____ Score_____	5th Try Date_____ Score_____
1	red	red	red	red	red
2	blue	blue	blue	blue	blue
3	yellow	yellow	yellow	yellow	yellow
4	green	green	green	green	green
5	purple	purple	purple	purple	purple
6	orange	orange	orange	orange	orange
7	brown	brown	brown	brown	brown
8	black	black	black	black	black
9	gray	gray	gray	gray	gray
10	white	white	white	white	white
11	one	one	one	one	one
12	two	two	two	two	two

(S)

13	three	three	three	three	three
14	four	four	four	four	four
15	five	five	five	five	five
16	six	six	six	six	six
17	seven	seven	seven	seven	seven
18	eight	eight	eight	eight	eight
19	nine	nine	nine	nine	nine
20	ten	ten	ten	ten	ten
21	eleven	eleven	eleven	eleven	eleven
22	twelve	twelve	twelve	twelve	twelve
23	thirteen	thirteen	thirteen	thirteen	thirteen
24	fourteen	fourteen	fourteen	fourteen	fourteen
25	fifteen	fifteen	fifteen	fifteen	fifteen
26	sixteen	sixteen	sixteen	sixteen	sixteen
27	seventeen	seventeen	seventeen	seventeen	seventeen
28	eighteen	eighteen	eighteen	eighteen	eighteen
29	nineteen	nineteen	nineteen	nineteen	nineteen
30	twenty	twenty	twenty	twenty	twenty

(S)

31	thirty	thirty	thirty	thirty	thirty
32	forty	forty	forty	forty	forty
33	fifty	fifty	fifty	fifty	fifty
34	sixty	sixty	sixty	sixty	sixty
35	seventy	seventy	seventy	seventy	seventy
36	eighty	eighty	eighty	eighty	eighty
37	ninety	ninety	ninety	ninety	ninety
38	hundred	hundred	hundred	hundred	hundred
39	thousand	thousand	thousand	thousand	thousand
40	million	million	million	million	million
41	January	January	January	January	January
42	February	February	February	February	February
43	March	March	March	March	March
44	April	April	April	April	April
45	May	May	May	May	May
46	June	June	June	June	June
47	July	July	July	July	July
48	August	August	August	August	August

(S)

49	September	September	September	September	September
50	October	October	October	October	October
51	November	November	November	November	November
52	December	December	December	December	December
53	Monday	Monday	Monday	Monday	Monday
54	Tuesday	Tuesday	Tuesday	Tuesday	Tuesday
55	Wednesday	Wednesday	Wednesday	Wednesday	Wednesday
56	Thursday	Thursday	Thursday	Thursday	Thursday
57	Friday	Friday	Friday	Friday	Friday
58	Saturday	Saturday	Saturday	Saturday	Saturday
59	Sunday	Sunday	Sunday	Sunday	Sunday

Student Test
1. Copy this test
2. Flag or protect to use again
3. Date & score tutor copy

Sight Words (S)

1	red
2	blue
3	yellow
4	green
5	purple
6	orange
7	brown
8	black
9	gray
10	white
11	one
12	two

(S)

13	three
14	four
15	five
16	six
17	seven
18	eight
19	nine
20	ten
21	eleven
22	twelve
23	thirteen
24	fourteen
25	fifteen
26	sixteen
27	seventeen
28	eighteen
29	nineteen
30	twenty

(S)

31	thirty
32	forty
33	fifty
34	sixty
35	seventy
36	eighty
37	ninety
38	hundred
39	thousand
40	million
41	January
42	February
43	March
44	April
45	May
46	June
47	July
48	August

(S)

49	September
50	October
51	November
52	December
53	Monday
54	Tuesday
55	Wednesday
56	Thursday
57	Friday
58	Saturday
59	Sunday

Tutor Copy
1. Copy this page
2. Mark missed words in **COLUMN #1** as student reads from student test
3. Find marked words & ask student to read words in columns #2-6
4. Note date and save page in binder
5. Use lesson plans to teach phonics concepts

6. Retest & reteach until mastery is reached

Phonics Test-Step 1 (P1)
Date:_____

	Test Word	2nd check...	3rd check...	4th check ...	5th check...	6th check ...	Teach Step 1 Lesson #
1	bag	am	cat	had	add	class	1- short a
2	beg	red	hen	end	fell	dress	2- short e
3	if	in	him	fill	kid	swim	3- short i
4	top	got	off	on	bog	fox	4- short o
5	up	bug	fun	truck	hug	much	5- short u
6	he	we	be	me			6- long e
7	so	go	no	old	cold	fold	7- long o
8	name	gave	late	rake	care	sale	8- a/ final e
9	here	these					9- e/ final e
10	five	nine	ride	white	smile	size	10- i/ final e
11	home	close	bone	rope	stole	nose	11- o/ final e
12	blue	true	rule	mule	cube	cute	12- u/ final e
13	bay	clay	day	may	ray	say	13- ay
14	rain	tail	again	bait	maid	claim	14- ai
15	see	tree	feel	feet	sleep	free	15- ee
16	lie	pie	tie	tied	cried	believe	16- ie

(P1)

17	road	toad	load	boat	coat	soak	17- oa
18	ear	fear	leave	team	weak	cheap	18- ea
19	out	our	house	round	cloud	mouth	19- ou
20	how	now	down	owl	flower	brown	20- ow
21	bow	tow	show	grow			21- ow= long o
22	too	soon	food	room	school		22- oo
23	boy	toy	joy	enjoy			23- oy
24	coin	join	boil	noise	point	voice	24- oi
25	new	dew	blew	grew	few	threw	25- ew
26	are	car	dark	hard	large	arm	26- ar
27	or	for	more	short	fork	sport	27- or
28	first	girl	bird	dirt	third	skirt	28- ir
29	turn	burn	hurt	during	hurry	return	29- ur
30	mother	ever	person	number	later	teacher	30- er
31	chip	chap	chat	chess	chase	cheap	31- ch
32	shack	sham	she	shame	shake	shape	32- sh
33	than	that	them	then	thick	thin	33- th
34	whack	wham	what	where	whim	whip	34- wh

(P1)

35	sack	pack	check	lick	sock	buck	35 –ck
36	bang	ding	anything	bong	song	lung	36 -ng
37	knack	knee	knew	knit	knock	knot	37- kn
38	comb	tomb	crumb				38 -mb
39	catch	match	itch	ditch	pitch	hutch	39 -tch
40	badge	pledge	lodge	budge	bridge		40 –dge
41	cage	giant	bridge	danger	gentle		41- soft g
42	ice	nice	face	cent	circle	center	42- soft c
43	bail	fail	nail	rail	snail	tail	43- ail
44	main	chain	gain	pain	stain	train	44- ain
45	air	chair	fair	hair	lair	pair	45- air
46	all	ball	call	mall	stall	tall	46- all
47	bare	care	dare	rare	scare	stare	47- are
48	fight	night	sight	tight	light	tonight	48- ight
49	itch	ditch	pitch	stitch	switch	hitch	49- itch
50	give	live	jive	live			50- ive
51	bone	cone	lone	stone	tone	zone	51- one
52	ought	bought	fought	sought	thought		52- ought

(P1)

53	cure	lure	pure	nature			53- ure
54	scab	scale	scan	scar	scum		54- sc
55	skate	skid	skill	skip	skull	sky	55- sk
56	smack	small	smart	smile	smoke	smug	56- sm
57	snack	snap	sniff	snob	snort	snug	57- sn
58	span	spat	speck	spill	spot	spurt	58- sp
59	strand	strap	straw	strict	stroke	strut	59- str
60	swam	swim	swum	sweet	swear	swish	60- sw
61	brace	brad	bran	bred	brick	brim	61- br
62	crab	crack	crazy	cream	crib	cry	62- cr
63	drab	drag	drift	drill	drop	drum	63- dr
64	grab	gram	gray	grew	grid	grunt	64- gr
65	prank	press	prim	prod	prop	prune	65- pr
66	trap	tray	tree	trick	trim	trot	66- tr
67	wrap	wren	wring	wrist	write	wrong	67- wr
68	black	blast	bless	blink	blob	blue	68- bl
69	clad	clam	clap	clean	cliff	clock	69- cl
70	flag	flap	fled	flick	flock	flower	70- fl

(P1)

71	plan	plant	pled	plop	pluck	plug	71- pl
72	slab	slam	sled	slit	slim	slum	72- sl
73	ask	bask	task	brisk	risk		73 –sk
74	clasp	rasp	grasp				74 –sp (ending)
75	fast	best	fist	bust	first	worst	75 –st (ending)
76	band	land	bend	send	bind	bond	76 –nd
77	bank	tank	ink	sink	bunk	trunk	77 –nk
78	ant	pant	rent	dint	mint	punt	78 –nt
79	age	rage	barge	fudge	bulge	range	79- ge (ending)
80	camp	ramp	crimp	limp	bump	stump	80 –mp

Student Test
1. Copy and save this page.
2. Student reads words.
3. Tutor scores tutor copy.
4. Give additional words from tutor copy if necessary.

Phonics Test- (P1)

1	bag
2	beg
3	if
4	top
5	up
6	he
7	so
8	name
9	here
10	five
11	home
12	blue

(P1)

13	bay
14	rain
15	see
16	lie
17	road
18	ear
19	out
20	how
21	bow
22	too
23	boy
24	coin
25	new
26	are
27	or
28	first
29	turn
30	mother

(P1)

31	chip
32	shack
33	than
34	whack
35	sack
36	bang
37	knack
38	comb
39	catch
40	badge
41	cage
42	ice
43	bail
44	main
45	air
46	all
47	bare
48	fight

(P1)

49	itch
50	give
51	bone
52	ought
53	cure
54	scab
55	skate
56	smack
57	snack
58	span
59	strand
60	swam
61	brace
62	crab
63	drab
64	grab
65	prank
66	trap

(P1)

67	wrap
68	black
69	clad
70	flag
71	plan
72	slab
73	ask
74	clasp
75	fast
76	band
77	bank
78	ant
79	age
80	camp

Tutor Copy

1. Copy this page
2. Mark missed words in **COLUMN #1** as student reads from student test
3. Find marked words & ask student to read words in columns #2-6
4. Note date and save page in binder
5. Use lesson plans to teach phonics concepts
6. Retest & reteach until mastery is reached

Phonics Test - Step 2 (P2)
Date:_____

	Test Word	2nd check...	3rd check...	4th check...	5th check...	6th check...	Teach Step 2 Lesson #
1	rag	fact	grasp	draft	grant	satisfy	81- short a
2	bet	tent	mend	gem	check	drench	82- short e
3	ink	lift	dim	rich	linen	riddle	83- short i
4	hog	crop	flop	proper	logic	solid	84- short o
5	bud	struck	lump	stuff	fund	plum	85- short u
6	skate	frame	snake	create	sane	inhale	86- a/ final e
7	eve	severe	supreme	scene	precede		87- e/ final e
8	pipe	dine	hire	polite	bribe	despite	88- i/ final e
9	stove	vote	cone	rose	zone	expose	89 - o/ final e
10	mule	June	cute	value	produce	assume	90- u/ final e
11	bay	payroll	delay	display	relay	halfway	91- ay
12	aim	gain	paint	faith	mail	remain	92- ai
13	reef	speed	steel	beef	speech	agree	93- ee
14	field	chief	niece	priest	fierce	frontier	94- ie
15	oats	toast	loaf	roast	roam	loan	95- oa
16	speak	beach	bead	tea	neat	tease	96- ea

(P2)

17	hour	mountain	wound	tough	outline	discount	97- ou
18	vowel	allow	crown	coward	sparrow	plow	98- ow= long o
19	soon	scooter	foolish	tooth	shampoo	smooth	99- oo
20	oyster	royal	employ	ploy			100- oy
21	choice	spoil	moist	appoint	avoid	moisture	101- oi
22	newspaper	knew	chew	view	chewy		102- ew
23	March	carpet	artist	tardy	depart	cargo	103- ar
24	border	porch	honor	ignore	force	oral	104- or
25	thirst	firm	Virginia				105- ir
26	curl	burst	fur	surf	survive	jury	106- ur
27	tender	folder	cover	verb	meter	shiver	107- er
28	chair	chamber	chatter	chief	childhood	chubby	108- ch
29	shortstop	shrink	shun	shutter	shrimp	shrivel	109- sh
30	theft	thermal	thicken	thrash	throb	thrust	110- th
31	wharf	whether	whichever	whomever	wholly	whiten	111- wh
32	rickrack	airsick	limerick	sidekick	deadlock	struck	112 –ck
33	slang	bullring	wellspring	headlong	lifelong	prolong	113 -ng
34	gnat	gnaw	gnome	gnu	gnarl		114- gn

(P2)

35	knapsack	knelt	knives	knoll	knotty	know-how	115- kn
36	pneumonia	pneumatic					116- pn
37	hymn	condemn	column				117- mn
38	patch	outmatch	unlatch	twitch	bewitch	butcher	118- tch
39	budget	knowledge	hodgepodge				119- dge
40	garage	damage	gentle	strange	imagine	energy	120- soft g
41	excited	notice	success	dancer	cereal	recent	121- soft c
42	airmail	bobtail	entail	hangnail	ponytail	prevail	122- ail
43	attain	detain	domain	explain	ordain	pertain	123- ain
44	armchair	despair	impair	wheelchair			124- air
45	baseball	coverall	downfall	install	overall	rainfall	125- all
46	aware	beware	compare	declare	hardware	nightmare	126- are
47	anyway	betray	freeway	hearsay	payday	portray	127- ay
48	fight	plight	delight	firefight	limelight	stoplight	128- ight
49	backstitch	bewitch	hemstitch	top stitch	unhitch		129- itch
50	connive	revive	survive	positive	creative	relative	130- ive
51	prone	backbone	condone	limestone	postpone	wishbone	131- one
52	ought	drought	sought				132- ought

(P2)

53	mature	secure	endure	adventure	furniture	temperature	133- ure
54	action	direction	nation	fiction	education	lotion	134- tion
55	decision	discussion	confusion	tension	vision	mission	135- sion
56	curious	serious	delicious				136- ious
57	generous	nervous	tremendous	humorous			137- ous
58	fence	difference	sequence				138- ence
59	glance	finance	fragrance	ignorance	entrance	resistance	139- ance
60	graph	triumph	phase	phone	photo	phrase	140- ph
61	billion	million	onion	companion	union	scallion	141- ion= yun
62	question	quick	quiz				142- qu= kwa

Student Test
1. Copy and save this page.
2. Student reads words.
3. Tutor scores tutor copy.
4. Give additional words from tutor copy if necessary.

Phonics Test (P2)

1	rag
2	bet
3	ink
4	hog
5	bud
6	skate
7	eve
8	pipe
9	stove
10	mule
11	bay
12	aim

(P2)

13	reef
14	field
15	oats
16	speak
17	hour
18	vowel
19	soon
20	oyster
21	choice
22	newspaper
23	March
24	border
25	thirst
26	curl
27	tender
28	chair
29	shortstop
30	theft

(P2)

31	wharf
32	rickrack
33	slang
34	gnat
35	knapsack
36	pneumonia
37	hymn
38	patch
39	budget
40	garage
41	excited
42	airmail
43	attain
44	armchair
45	baseball
46	aware
47	anyway
48	fight

(P2)

49	backstitch
50	connive
51	prone
52	ought
53	mature
54	action
55	decision
56	curious
57	generous
58	fence
59	glance
60	graph
61	billion
62	question

Tutor Copy

1. Copy this page
2. Mark missed words in **COLUMN #1** as student reads from student test
3. Find marked words & ask student to read words in columns #2-6
4. Note date and save page in binder
5. Use lesson plans to teach phonics concepts
6. Retest & reteach until mastery is reached

Phonics Test- Step 3 (P3)
Date:_____

	Test Word	2nd Check	3rd Check...	4th Check ..	5th Check...	6th Check ..	Teach Step 3 Lesson #
1	gale	create	share	educate	inhale	sane	143- long a
2	severe	hemisphere	supreme				144- long e
3	describe	excite	polite	admire	bribe	empire	145- long i
4	tone	stroke	telescope	globe	zone	expose	146- long o
5	rescue	volume	issue	dispute	scuba	assume	147- long u
6	layer	essay	decay	frayed	portray	delay	148- ay
7	aid	gait	failure	plain	despair	frail	149- ai
8	keel	leer	leech	freedom	committee	sneeze	150- ee
9	shield	shriek	relieve	frontier	belief	grief	151- ie
10	goal	boast	cocoa	approach	coast		152- oa
11	cease	reveal	defeat	impeach	features	reappear	153- ea
12	trout	pouch	announce	encounter	council	pout	154- ou
13	owner	burrow					155- ow= long o
14	drowsy	towering	Mayflower				156- ow
15	booming	nook	textbook	groove	bamboo	moody	157- oo
16	loyal	destroy	boycott	convoy	royalty		158- oy

(P3)

17	hoist	avoid	appoint	recoil	rejoice	boisterous	159- oi
18	news	view	chewy				160- ew
19	arch	barter	charter	remark	molar	snarl	161- ar
20	forced	ordinary	nor	vigor	perform	portrait	162- or
21	circumstance						163- ir
22	urge	urban	rural	surplus	current	pluralism	164- ur
23	terms	perk	merchant	derby	concern	avert	165- er
24	champagne	chancellor	chaplain	chassis	chasm	crochet	166- soft ch
25	chemical	chlorine	chromosome	trachea	mechanism		167- hard ch
26	shellac	shepherd	sherbert	sheriff	Shinto	shortening	168- sh
27	thyme	thereafter	thesaurus				169- th
28	whether	whichever	wholesome	whiten			170- wh
29	gnat	gnaw	gnome	gnu	gnarl		171- gn
30	knelt	knicknack	knighthood	knives	knoll	knowledge	172- kn
31	pneumonia	pneumatic					173- pn
32	hymn	condemn	column				174- mn
33	twitch	backstitch	outmatch	bewitch	unhitch	butcher	175- tch
34	knowledge	budget	hodgepodge				176- dge

(P3)

35	bulge	margin	generally	rigid	passage	legend	177- soft g
36	cycle	civil	cancel	innocent	precise	ceremony	178- soft c
37	travail	airmail	ponytail				179- ail
38	ascertain	abstain	attain				180- ain
39	armchair	despair	impair	wheelchair			181- air
40	appall	forestall	baseball				182- all
41	threadbare	welfare	declare				183- are
42	stoplight	limelight	alright				184- ight
43	unhitch	top stitch	bewitch				185- itch
44	relative	connive	positive	progressive			186- ive
45	telephone	enthrone	cortisone				187- one
46	ought	sought	drought				188- ought
47	furniture	endure	secure				189- ure
48	function	infection	tradition	section	inspection	destination	190- tion
49	tension	dimension	version	admission	invasion	mansion	191- sion
50	furious	mysterious	glorious	spacious	precious	luscious	192- ious
51	enormous	numerous	miraculous	monotonous	prosperous		193- ous
52	residence	coincidence	consequence	reference			194- ence
53	France	romance	prance	finance	tolerance	defiance	195- ance

Student Test

1. Copy and save this page.
2. Student reads words.
3. Tutor scores tutor copy.
4. Give additional words from tutor copy if necessary.

Phonics Test (P3)

1	gale
2	severe
3	describe
4	tone
5	rescue
6	layer
7	aid
8	keel
9	shield
10	goal
11	cease
12	trout

(P3)

13	owner
14	drowsy
15	booming
16	loyal
17	hoist
18	news
19	arch
20	forced
21	circumstance
22	urge
23	terms
24	champagne
25	chemical
26	shellac
27	thyme
28	whether
29	gnat
30	knelt

(P3)

31	pneumonia
32	hymn
33	twitch
34	knowledge
35	bulge
36	cycle
37	travail
38	ascertain
39	armchair
40	appall
41	threadbare
42	stoplight
43	unhitch
44	relative
45	telephone
46	ought
47	furniture
48	function

(P3)

49	tension
50	furious
51	enormous
52	residence
53	France

Notes about Fluency Tests

Use these keys to help you understand which sight words your child needs to learn. You will also find information to help you pinpoint which phonics lessons to teach.

SE1 = Sight Words Step 1 (Early 1st Grade)
SML1 = Sight Words Step 1 (Middle & Late 1st Grade)
S2 = Sight Words Step 1 (2nd Grade)
S34 = Sight Words Step 2 (3rd & 4th Grade)
S100 = 100 Most Common Sight Words
S = Colors, Numbers, Months, Days of the Week

There are more fluency tests for Step 1 for a simple reason: there are more phonics concepts and sight words to master when first learning to read. Many of the phonics lessons found in Steps 2 and 3 build on basic rules learned in Step 1. The words are simply longer, often combining two or more phonics lessons. The early fluency tests provide more word information for the same reason. In later fluency tests, you will be more concerned with speed, intonation, etc. and have to worry less about, say, short a vowel sounds.

If your child finishes a paragraph before the one minute timer, instruct her to keep going by starting over.

Remember, don't give these tests so often that your child memorizes them!

Tutor Copy
1. Copy appropriate fluency tests.
2. Set timer for 60 seconds.
3. Score this copy as student reads from *student* test.
4. Date and score.
5. Practice fluency, phonics and sight words.

6. Retest until grade-level mastery is reached.

Fluency Test Step 1 (Early 1ˢᵗ Grade) (FE1)

I run to the bus. My dog is with   9
  SEI short u SE1 SE1   Short u   SME1   Short o SEI SE1

me. My dog can not go! I stop. I   18
SML1   SML1   short o   SE1   SE1 SML1   SE1 short o   SE1

say, "No, Spot! You are a   dog!   25
 SE1   long o Short o   SE1   SE1   SE1   Short o

Why do you want to go with me?"   33
SML1   SE1 SE1   SML1   SE1 SML1 SE1   SML1

I tell him to go back home. He   41
SE1 Short e SE1   SE1   SML1   short a   SML1/long o   SE1

can play with Mom or the cat.   48
SE1   ay   SE1   Short o   SE1 SE1   Short a

He can eat lunch and look at   55
SE1   SE1   ea   short u   SE1   SE1   short a

the moon. Spot walks home to   61
SE1   oo   Short o   SML1   long o/e   SE1

play ball. I see him go. I think   69
ay   all   SE1 ee   SE1   SME1   SE1 SME1

Spot is a good dog.   74
short o   SE1 SE1   oo   short o

Student Test
1. Copy this test
2. Flag or protect to use again
3. Date & score tutor copy

Fluency Test (FE1)

I run to the bus. My dog is with me. My dog can not go! I stop. I say, "No, Spot! You are a dog! Why do you want to go with me?" I tell him to go back home. He can play with Mom or the cat. He can eat lunch and look at the moon. Spot walks home to play ball. I see him go. I think Spot is a good dog.

Fluency Test - Step 1 (Middle 1ˢᵗ Grade) (FM1)

Where is my green bike? I want   7

SML1   SE1 SML1   ee   long i/e   SE1 SML1

to ride it! It is not near our house.   16

SE1 Long i/e SE1 SE1 SE1 SE1   ea   SML1

I can't find it. I must find it, but it   26

SE1 Contraction SML1 SE1 SE1 SE1   SML1   SE1 SE1 SE1

is gone. I ask my mother if she has   35

SE1   SE1 SML1 SML1   SE1   SE1

seen my bike. She says no. I ask   43

ee   SML1   long i/e   SML1   long o SE1 SML1

my dad. He doesn't know where   49

SML1 Short a   SE1   Contraction   SML1   SML1

my new bike is. I am mad. My   57

SML1 SML1   Long i/e SE1   SE1 Short a Short a   SML1

dog, Spot, barks at me. He jumps   64

short o   short o   ar   Short a SE1   SE1   short u

up and looks at his dish. Water!   71

SE1   SE1   SE1/ oo   short a SE1   Short I   SML1

I put my bike in the shed out of the   81

SE1 SML1   SML1   long i/e SE1 SE1 short e/sh SE1   SE1 SE1

rain. I laugh because Spot is smart.   88

ai   SE1   SML1   Short o SE1 ar

He knows where to find my bike.   95

SE1   SML1   SML1   SE1   SML1 long i/e

Student Test

1. Copy this test
2. Flag or protect to use again

3. Date & score tutor copy

Fluency Test (FM1)

Where is my green bike? I want to ride it! It is not near our house. I can't find it. I must find it, but it is gone. I ask my mother if she has seen my bike. She says no. I ask my dad. He doesn't know where my new bike is. I am mad. My dog, Spot, barks at me. He jumps up and looks at his dish. Water! I put my bike in the shed out of the rain. I laugh because Spot is smart. He knows where to find my bike!

Fluency Test - Step 1 (Late 1ˢᵗ Grade) (FL1)

My sister is a baby. My mother 　　7
SML1　　　　SE1 SE1 Long a　　SML1

says, "Nap time!" and my sister 　　13
SML1　　Short a　long i/e　　SE1　SE1

takes a nap. She likes to sleep, but 　　21
long a/e　SE1 short a　　long i/e SE1　ee　　SE1

I do not like naps at all. I leave the 　　31
SE1 SE1　SE1　long i/e　short a　short a SE1　SE1　ea　SE1

room. I will never go to bed! I play 　　40
oo　　SE1　SE1　　SML1 SE1　short e　SE1 ay

a game with my friend. I drop a 　　48
SE1 long a/e　SE1　SML1　　　SE1 short o　SE1

rock in the water. I put a yellow 　　56
short o　SE1 SE1　　SE1 SML1 SE1　S

basket on my bike. I run with my 　　64
short a/short e　SE1　SML1 long i/e　SE1 short u SE1　SML1

orange and blue flag. I kick a can 　　72
S　SE1　S　Short a　SE1 short i　SE1　short a

around my street. Now, I am tired. 　　79
SML1　SML1　ee　SML1　SE1 short a long i/e

My bed looks good. Maybe 　　84
SML1　short e SE1　oo　SML1

I should take a nap today. 　　90
SE1　long a/e SE1 short a

Student Test
1. Copy this test
2. Flag or protect to use again
3. Date & score tutor copy

Fluency Test (FL1)

My sister is a baby. My mother says, "Nap time!" and my sister takes a nap. She likes to sleep, but I do not like naps at all. I leave the room. I will never go to bed! I play a game with my friend. I drop a rock in the water. I put a yellow basket on my bike. I run with my orange and blue flag. I kick a can around my street. Now, I *am* tired. My bed looks good. Maybe I should take a nap today.

Tutor Copy
1. Copy appropriate fluency tests.
2. Set timer for 60 seconds.
3. Circle misread words as student reads from *student* test.
4. Date and score.
5. Practice fluency, phonics and sight words.

6. Retest until grade-level mastery is reached.

Fluency Test- Step 1 (2nd Grade) (F2)

I write my Grandmother a letter	6
<small>wr short a/ er S2</small>	
every week. I tell her what I have	14
<small>S2 ee short e SE1</small>	
learned in school, answer her	19
<small>S2 sc/ oo S2</small>	
questions, and thank her for the	25
<small>qu=kwa th/short a/-nk</small>	
twenty dollars she sent me for my	32
<small>short e dbl cons short e SML2</small>	
birthday. On the last page, I draw a	40
<small>ir/ ay short a S2/ soft g aw</small>	
picture of America. It is time for	47
<small>S2/ ure S2 long i/e</small>	
dinner, so I end my letter. I put it in	57
<small>dbl cons/ er short e S2</small>	
an envelope with a thirty cent stamp	64
<small>short e/ long e/e th/ ir soft c st/ -mp</small>	
in the right corner. I go outside and	72
<small>ight hard c/ er ou/ long i/e</small>	
mail the letter. I hope my	78
<small>ai S2 long o/e</small>	
grandmother likes it.	81
<small>Short a/ er long i/ e</small>	

Student Test
1. Copy this test
2. Flag or protect to use again
3. Date & score tutor copy

Fluency Test (F2)

I write my Grandmother a letter every week. I tell her what I have learned in school, answer her questions, and thank her for the twenty dollars she sent me for my birthday. On the last page, I draw a picture of America. It is time for dinner, so I end my letter. I put it in an envelope with a thirty cent stamp in the right corner. I go outside and mail the letter. I hope my grandmother likes it.

Tutor Copy
1. Copy appropriate fluency tests.
2. Set timer for 60 seconds.
3. Circle misread words as student reads from *student* test.
4. Date and score.
5. Practice fluency, phonics and sight words.

6. Retest until grade-level mastery is reached.

Fluency Test Step 2 (3rd Grade) (F3)

Last June my family went on a	7
trip to the mountains. We left early <small>long u/e/S S3</small>	14
in the morning. It was still dark <small>S3/ ou</small>	21
outside. There were no lights on in <small>ar</small>	28
the city. It felt like the whole earth <small>ight</small>	36
was still asleep! My father says that <small>S3 wh/ Long o/e S3</small>	43
it is important for children to travel <small>ee</small>	50
and see new things. What a vacation! <small>S3 S3</small>	57
My brother and I found a sparrow's nest <small>long a/ tion</small> <small>ou ow</small>	65

(F3)

and an Indian arrowhead. We ate   71
     S3   ow/ ea

oysters at a restaurant. We saw a   78
oy/ er

billion stars! We had a really super   85
ion=yun   ar   S34   long u/e

time! My family didn't want to leave!   92
     S34   S34

Student Test
1. Copy this test
2. Flag or protect to use again
3. Date & score tutor copy

Fluency Test (F3)

Last June my family went on a trip to the mountains. We left early in the morning. It was still dark outside. There were no lights on in the city. It felt like the whole earth was still asleep! My father says that it is important for children to travel and see new things. What a vacation! My brother and I found a sparrow's nest and an Indian arrowhead. We ate oysters at a restaurant. We saw a billion stars! We had a really super time! My family didn't want to leave!

Tutor Copy
1. Copy appropriate fluency tests.
2. Set timer for 60 seconds.
3. Circle misread words as student reads from *student* test.
4. Date and score.
5. Practice fluency, phonics and sight words.

6. Retest until grade-level mastery is reached.

Fluency Test Step 2 (4th Grade) (F4)

I am so excited! My sister is in big trouble!	10
This is what happened. My mom was Soft c	17
sitting in her armchair reading the newspaper.	24
My father was sick in bed with pneumonia. ar/ air	32
I was in my room talking on the telephone. pn/ eu	41
Suddenly, we heard an explosion. I ph	47
thought it was a bomb! We all ran down sion	56
the hallway and opened the front door. mb	63
We found my sister sitting in the driveway all/ ay S34	71
looking foolish. She had backed the S2/ ou long e/ ay	77
car into the garage! After much discussion, oo	84

S34   Soft g   sion

(F4)

my parents decided that my sister has to   92

Soft c

get a job and pay for the damage to the   102

Soft g

car and the house. I think she ought to   111

S2   ought

buy us a new house for a million dollars!   120

ion=yun

Student Test
1. Copy this test
2. Flag or protect to use again
3. Date & score tutor copy

Fluency Test (F4)

I am so excited! My sister is in big trouble! This is what happened. My mom was sitting in her armchair reading the newspaper. My father was sick in bed with pneumonia. I was in my room talking on the telephone. Suddenly, we heard an explosion. I thought it was a bomb! We all ran down the hallway and opened the front door. We found my sister sitting in the driveway looking foolish. She had backed the car into the garage! After much discussion, my parents decided that my sister has to get a job and pay for the damage to the car and the house. I think she ought to buy us a new house for a million dollars!

Fluency Test - Step 3 (5th Grade) (F5)

I am a magnificent cook. Alright, maybe I   8
<small>soft c   ight</small>

exaggerate. I am a really, really good cook. I am very   19
<small>Soft g</small>

creative. My knowledge of cooking styles is extensive.   27
<small>ive   dge</small>

So imagine how I rejoiced when the local cooking school   37
<small>soft g   oi</small>

announced that they were having a Cook Off. I knew that   48
<small>soft c</small>

I would win the grand prize. Failure was not an option.   59
<small>   ai   tion</small>

Nobody could defeat or outmatch me. On the day of the   70
<small>   ea   tch</small>

competition, I decided to make my eight layer onion   79
<small>tion   soft c   S   ay   ion=yun</small>

cherry cake. While I waited for the cake to cook, I   90

watched the other cooks perform. Poor things, I wanted   99

to rescue them. Finally it was time to share my creation,   110

but something was wrong. I had forgotten to turn on the   121
<small>   wr</small>

(F5)

oven! The temperature was zero degrees! I didn't have   130

cake, I had soup! I felt queasy. My humiliation was   140
_{ure}   _{ee}

complete. I served my creation anyway, and guess what   149
   _{qu=kwa}   _{tion}

happened? The judges pounced on my soup, and I won   159
     _{tion}

1st prize! It was miraculous! Triumph!   165
           _{ou}
              _{ous}   _{ph}

Fluency Test (F5)

I am a magnificent cook. Alright, maybe I exaggerate. I am a really, really good cook. I am creative. My knowledge of cooking styles is extensive. So imagine how I rejoiced when the local cooking school announced that they were having a Cook Off. I knew that I would win the grand prize. Failure was not an option. Nobody could defeat or outmatch me. On the day of the competition, I decided to make my eight layer onion cherry cake. While I waited for the cake to cook, I watched the other cooks perform. Poor things, I wanted to rescue them. Finally it was time to share my creation, but something was wrong. I had forgotten to turn on the oven!

(F5)

The temperature was zero degrees! I didn't have cake, I had soup! I felt queasy. My humiliation was complete. I served my creation anyway, and guess what happened? The judges pounced on my soup, and I won 1st prize! It was miraculous! Triumph!

Tutor Copy
1. Copy appropriate fluency tests.
2. Set timer for 60 seconds.
3. Circle misread words as student reads from *student* test.
4. Date and score.
5. Practice fluency, phonics and sight words.

6. Retest until grade-level mastery is reached.

Fluency Test- Step 3 (6th Grade) (F6)

Last month I began to feel very peculiar. I became   10

drowsy in the middle of the afternoon, I had no tolerance   21
ar

for my favorite foods, and I started to look like a frail   33
ow ance

gnome. My mother said, "Maybe you have a parasite."   42
ai

My brother recoiled and screamed, "Stay away! You   50
gn

might be contagious!" My mother took me to the doctor.   60
oi

The doctor studied my blood under a telescope; she poked   70
ious

at my features; and she did other explorations that I do not   82

wish to discuss. "You will be relieved to know that your   93
tion

sickness is not imaginary," she said. "I have ascertained   102
ie

that you have an obscure but primitive disease. Only a   112
soft g ain
ure ive

(F6)

chemist such as myself, with amazing intelligence could   120
ch=k   soft g, soft c

diagnose your disease. The treatment is controversial, but   128

I guarantee that you will be cured." I have spent the last   139

few weeks sitting under artificial lights and eating   147
                              soft c

chocolate sundaes precisely every four hours.   153
soft c   S

Student Test
1. Copy this test
2. Flag or protect to use again
3. Date & score tutor copy

Fluency Test (F6)

Last month I began to feel very peculiar. I became drowsy in the middle of the afternoon, I had no tolerance for my favorite foods, and I started to look like a frail gnome. My mother said, "Maybe you have a parasite." My brother recoiled and screamed, "Stay away! You might be contagious!" My mother took me to the doctor. The doctor studied my blood under a telescope; she poked at my features; and she did other explorations that I do not wish to discuss. "You will be relieved to know that your sickness is not imaginary," she said. "I have ascertained that you have an obscure but primitive disease. Only a chemist such as myself, with amazing intelligence could diagnose your disease. The treatment is controversial, but I guarantee that you will be cured." I have spent the last few weeks sitting under artificial lights and eating chocolate sundaes precisely every four hours.

PART THREE

TEACH THEM WHAT THEY DON'T KNOW

CHAPTER 9

LESSONS

Finally! It's tutoring time! After completing the sight word, phonics and fluency assessments, you know exactly which words and concepts to teach. You know how many correct words per minute (CWPM) your child reads and if this number is above or below grade-level. With such detailed information, you understand more about your child's reading situation than most parents, and, sadly, many of their teachers.

There are thousands of games, ideas, websites and books to help you teach sight words, phonics and fluency. Frankly, it can be overwhelming! The lessons in <u>Tutor Your Child to Reading Success</u> have been selected for three reasons: they are fun for kids, easy for parents to teach, and, most importantly, they work. I show parents how to teach sight words, phonics and fluency by using the lessons and methods that I used in my classrooms and in my private tutoring business. Parents do not need to reinvent the wheel; the lessons can be used just as they are explained in the book. Of course, you are free to modify the lessons or create ones of your own. Ask other parents to share their best reading games or tips.

You may be surprised that there are only three or four basic lessons used to teach sight word and phonics. Children crave routine, and they respond to repetition. I used the same lessons, games and ideas over and over again, week after week. In fact, if I replaced Thursday's regular spelling game with a new one, my students revolted! Please don't think that you have to find new teaching ideas for *every* lesson. Find a few lessons that work, and stick with them!

Researchers have found that there are different types of learning styles, and not everybody learns best by sitting still and listening to the teacher talk. Nowadays, children are taught math from a number of different angles: listening to the teacher explain a concept, playing with blocks and other manipulatives, solving puzzles, writing on white boards, memorizing a poem, acting in a play. The more senses you can engage, the faster learning takes place. This explains why it is so much easier and more enjoyable to learn a new recipe while taking a hands-on cooking class than by reading a cookbook or listening to a lecture. Keep this in mind as you teach sight word, phonics and fluency lessons. Get your child moving, writing, singing, coloring, copying, memorizing, shuffling, searching, answering and laughing. More fun and less boredom means a better experience for both tutor and student.

Let's start teaching and learning!

CHAPTER *10*

HOW TO TEACH SIGHT WORDS

Learning sight words is crucial to your child's reading success, but teaching sight words does not have to be difficult. One of the best tools for teaching sight words are flash cards. In my opinion, flash cards are one of the best teaching tools ever invented. They are portable, adaptable, and inexpensive. I play games with flash cards, hide them around the house, tape them to doors and walls, and stick them to the refrigerator. I first fell in love with flash cards when my daughter was three. We made simple flash cards by gluing pictures from magazines and photos onto 3 X 5 cards. I wrote the name next to each picture. Some of these words were sight words like *house*, while others, like *pancakes* and *rabbit*, were important words in our family! Everyone was amazed at how many words my daughter learned to recognize.

You can buy preprinted flash cards in teacher stores, the big box stores, and even some grocery stores. You can get a free download of all the sight words in this book at my website: www.NatomasTutoring.com.

While it is easier to use pre-made flash cards, I strongly recommend that you and your child make some sets yourselves. Paying close attention to each new word, carefully writing each letter, repeating the word over and over- all of these things do wonders for learning and recall. For your very first sight word lesson, you and your child will create two sets of sight word flash cards.

Keep these things in mind when making flash cards:
- ✔ Write in black pen or marker. You want your son to be able to see the words from across the room or from the back seat of the car.
- ✔ Write clearly in the middle of the flash card.
- ✔ Write in manuscript (print), not cursive.
- ✔ Write in all lowercase letters- except "I" or a proper noun.
- ✔ Repeat each letter slowly as you write it.

Flash Cards

🏁 1. Ready- CHOOSE A LIST OF SIGHT WORDS & GATHER SUPPLIES

Find the first sight word assessment test you gave your son, Step 1 Early 1st Grade (I know it is in your tutoring binder!). Make a list of the words that he misread. You will use these words for your first sight word lessons.

For most sight word lessons, you will need:

> Blank 3 X 5 cards
> Flash Cards (made previously)
> Copies of Game Boards
> Markers, pen, pencil

2. On Your Marks- START TALKING

Choose the first word from your sight word list. (We will use *said*.)

> Say, "Remember last week when you read all of those sight words? You sure knew a lot of them, but I think it's time you learned all of them! What do you think about that? Do you think that you can learn five new sight words this week? We might decide that you can learn more than five, but let's start with that and see how it goes, okay? Here's the first word, *said*."

3. Get Set- MODEL

Show your son how to make a flash card.
> Say, "Watch me while I write each letter, s-a-i-d. Said. Say that for me. Good. Now, you write *said* on your own flash card."

4. Go! YOUR CHILD LEARNS

Give your son a 3 X 5 card and a pencil. Draw a line in the middle of the card so that his words will be centered and straight. Put your *said* flash card where he can *easily* see it. Say each letter and then wait while he writes it down neatly. Remind him not to write too small, but to use the entire center of the flash card.

> When he is finished, say, "Great job! Now, what is this word? *Said*, that's right! Take a good look at that word because you are going to see it all over the place! It's a sight word, which means that you shouldn't spend time sounding it out. You just have to know it when you see it. Can you think of a way to remember this word?"

The two of you brainstorm ideas to help him remember the word. It could be something as simple as *said starts with an s*. The more time you spend looking at, discussing, saying, and spelling a word, the faster your son will learn it.

When it comes to teaching and learning sight words, review and repetition are your best friends. Marketing experts tell us that we need to be exposed to information at least seven times before it actually sinks in. This explains why you see the same television commercials over and over again - they are trying to get that information into your head so you will finally buy their products. Children need to see sight words over and over and over again before the words sink in and can be read on sight. Before you make new flash cards, review the ones from days prior.

The temptation, especially if you feel that your son needs to learn a lot of sight words, is to make as many flash cards as possible in a short amount of time. I recommend limiting the number of new sight words and flash cards to *no more than three* a day. It is better for your child to master one or two sight words a day than to cram in and forget a half dozen.

There are so many things to do with your two sets of flash cards:

✔ Always keep one set in the binder or tote bag. The other set of flash cards can be put on the refrigerator in a special area cleared for just this purpose. Your son will walk by the fridge and read his sight words with pride and glee. Ah, sneaky teaching at its best!

✔ Once in a while, ask your son to read all of the words in a specified amount of time (say, 30 seconds). Keep the same time even as new words are added.

✔ Hide flash cards throughout the house: bathroom, dresser drawer, hamper. Your son earns points when he brings a card to you and reads it correctly.

Redeem the points at the end of the week. For example, 10 points earns 10 extra minutes before bedtime. You had better believe your son will be looking all over the house for those flash cards!

✔ Keep a set of flash cards in the car. Turn off the radio and ask your son to read the cards as fast as he can a few times. Or, the passenger (not the driver!) can hold up one flash card at a time while your son reads them from the back seat.

Sight Word Games

Memory

My favorite sight word game is the old game, Memory. Children adore it! I play Memory with sight words, spelling words, phonics- anything!

🏴 1. Ready- CHOSE SIGHT WORD CARDS

You need at least twenty flash cards (10 words) to make the game interesting and last more than 30 seconds! Depending on how fast you have been introducing sight words, it might take a while to acquire that many. Don't worry, your son can still enjoy playing Memory from the first day: make sight word flash cards from words that your son already knows. A little review never hurt anybody. Better yet, choose words that your son can read correctly but only after looking at them for a while. Hopefully, you took my advice and wrote down this information while doing sight word assessments. Playing games will give him the opportunity to learn these sight words with automaticity, immediate recognition.

Mix up the flash cards and place them facedown on the table.

2. On Your Marks- START TALKING

The object of the game is to find the cards that match. The purpose of the game is for your son to learn sight words.

> Say, "Have you ever played Memory before? It's easy! The object of the game is to find cards that have the same sight word on them. That's called making a match. A player can

only turn over two cards during his turn. If the cards match, the player puts them into his pile, scores a point and goes again. If the cards don't match, the player turns them back over, and the next player tries to find a match. Understand? Oh, and there is one more thing: *when you turn a card over, you have to read the word on it correctly or you lose your turn.*"

3. Get Set- MODEL

Go first. Turn over a card and read it, *was*. Turn over another card, *because*.

Say, "Oh, they don't match! Your turn!"

Turn both cards back over. Once in a while, purposely mispronounce a word and let your son correct you. Not only will he be thrilled, he will pay super-close attention to *every* sight word card you read!

4. Go! YOUR CHILD LEARNS

Continue the game. Your son turns over a card and reads the word, *because*. He remembers where to find the other *because,* turns it over and makes a match! He moves the two cards to his pile and takes another turn.

Remember, if your son misreads a card, he must turn in back over, even if he has a match.

Say, "Oh! You were so close, but that word is pronounced *yellow*! I know the next time you'll get it!"

Believe me, he'll know that word the next time.

Let's Make Sentences!

1. Ready- CHOOSE SIGHT WORD CARDS

Sight words may be learned individually, but, ultimately, your son will read them within sentences. This fun game helps your child combine sight words to express complete thoughts.

Place all of your flash cards face up on the table.

2. On Your Marks- START TALKING

Say, "You sure have been learning a lot of new sight words! Let's see if we can put them together and make them mean something! I'll go first..."

3. Get Set- MODEL

Look over all the sight word flash cards. Choose three or four to make a sentence. Lay the cards next to one another. Put your finger under each flash card as you read it out loud.

the. boy. was. little.

Repeat, saying the words faster so that they sound like a sentence.

"The boy was little. The boy was little!"

4. Go! YOUR CHILD LEARNS

Remove one card from the sentence and find another sight word flash card. Put the cards in order, and ask your son to read the new sentence. Keep your finger under the cards as he reads them. In the beginning, he may not read the words as a complete thought, but he will catch on soon.

the. girl. was. little. the. girl. was. little.

"The girl was little! The girl was little!"

Say, "Wow! You are reading!"

Let him repeat the sentence a few times before you change the sentence completely.

Keep this game in mind as you chose sight words from your list to teach. Here are the sentences my four-year old and I made with only his first nine sight word flash cards:

Come out.
Come out little boy.
Come out little girl.
The boy said come.
The girl said come.
The little boy said come.
The little girl said come.

The girl was out.

The boy was out.

The little boy was out.

The little girl was out.

The boy said go.

The girl said go.

The boy was little.

The girl was little.

Go boy.

Go girl.

Go little boy.

Go little girl.

Come girl.

Come boy.

Come little boy.

Come little girl.

Go boy said the little girl.

Go girl said the little boy.

Go little boy said the girl.

Go little girl said the boy.

Come said the girl.

Come said the boy.

Come said the little girl.

Come said the little boy.

I wanted to cry tears of joy when my son said, "I need *and*!" He realized that with one word he would be able to make a lot more sentences. When children ask for more information to solve problems or fill in the gaps of learning, it is called *discovery learning*. This is, arguably, the best kind of learning of all because the child is seeking information, hungry for knowledge. I realized that my son had nearly learned the word as he waited for me to write it on the flash card! He grabbed the flash card and was off!

Tic-Tac-Toe

Another game that I love to play with my students is Tic-Tac-Toe. It is quick to learn, fast and easy to play, can be played almost anywhere, and never gets boring. Most of us are familiar with this strategy game, and it is just as much fun as a learning game. Kids are so pleased and proud of themselves when they beat you - and they will! I have included some blank Tic-Tac-Toe game grids (see **Appendix Part 3 LESSONS**) to copy and keep ready for a quick game. If you would like to reuse a game board, put it in a plastic page protec-tor and use dry erase markers. Or, use beans, beads, or slips of paper instead of writing X's and O's. Use mark-and-erase or chalk boards, scribble on the back of an envelope or a piece of recycled paper- nearly anything will work!

🏳️ *1. Ready- CHOSE SIGHT WORDS*

Tic-Tac-Toe is a great way to review the sight words your child has already learned as well as teach new words. Mix old and new sight words. Use words from different lists (100 Most Common Sight Words and Step 2, for example).

Copy or make a Tic-Tac-Toe game board.

2. On Your Marks- START TALKING

The object of the game is to place three markers in row- vertically, horizon-tally or diagonally- while using strategy to prevent one's opponent from doing the same.

> Say, "Let's play a fun game called Tic-Tac-Toe. Usually, when you play this game, all you have to do is put your mark in a box and try to get three in a row. But, we are going to make it more interesting! For our game, *you have to correctly read the word in the box before you can put your mark down!*"

3. Get Set and Go! - PLAY THE GAME

Once in a while, draw a blank Tic-Tac-Toe board and give it to your child to fill with the words you have been studying. He will get a kick out of being the teacher, and you will enjoy watching him first intently consider which sight words to choose and then carefully write in each box.

Putting It All Together

Older children understandably resent being asked to play baby games, and some games are too difficult for younger children. I recommend Memory and Tic-Tac-Toe because both games are fun and appropriate for all grade levels. Begin each tutoring session with 15 minutes of sight words. Here's an easy plan:

> Introduce two new sight words by making flash cards.
> Play Memory.
> Play two games of Tic-Tac-Toe.

CHAPTER *11*

HOW TO TEACH PHONICS

Sight words, as I am sure you are tired of hearing, must be memorized. Most other words, thankfully, follow basic phonics rules. Once a child learns a phonics rule, she will then use it to read similar words. Of course, there is a small catch: our brains are not rule makers, but pattern detectors (Cunningham 1995). Simply being told a phonics rule will not help us magically read words using it. We need to see the phonics concept used over and over and over again until our brain forgets the rule and automatically recognizes the pattern.

When teaching phonics, you will introduce a rule or concept, and then share words with your child that use the concept over and over and over again. I have found that three or four tutoring sessions is usually all it takes to really drive home a new phonics lesson. With a lot of reading practice, the new phonics concept will soon become internalized- exactly what we want!

There is a special phonics lingo, but I believe that you can teach phonics without knowing or using the terminology. For example, you can teach Lesson 22 completely and successfully without ever having to say the word *dipthong*- or even know what it means! However, there is nothing wrong with looking in the Glossary and Definitions for a basic understanding of what you will be teaching.

Introducing a Phonics Lesson

1. *Ready*- MAKE COPIES AND CHOSE A PHONICS LESSON

Before teaching a new phonics lesson, look in **Appendix Part 3 LES-SONS** and make copies of the following:

      Phonics Introduction Page
      Tic-Tac-Toe Game Board
      Word Wheels

You will also need:

    Scored Phonics assessments

    3 X 5 cards

    Flash Cards to review

    Markers, pens, pencils, crayons, brads

Look at the first phonics assessment, Phonics Test Step 1, you gave your daughter. Find the rows in which she missed two or more words. These are the phonics lessons she needs to learn. We will use Lesson 25 Step 1/ *ew* as an example. Look in **Appendix Part 3 LESSONS** to find Lesson 25. Keep the book open and near you so that you can see it easily.

Both the tutor and the student will have a Phonics Introduction page for each phonics lesson. You will use this page to introduce a phonics rule or pattern (hence, the name). You will work with and refer to the Phonics Introduction Page throughout the week- reviewing words, drawing pictures, writing sentences- so keep it handy. Tutors write neatly in dark pen; students neatly copy in pencil.

2. On Your Marks- START TALKING

You say, "You have been doing such an amazing job learning sight words! I think we are ready to learn some other types of words, too! These words can be much easier to learn because you can sound them out! Isn't that great? Remember when I asked you to read that list of words last week? Well, I was looking at it today, and I saw that you were having trouble reading some of the *ew* words. So, I decided that it would be a good idea to start with Lesson 25."

3. Get Set and Go!

Write Lesson # 25 on the tutor Phonics Introduction Page and say, "Okay, you write that, too."

Your daughter writes Lesson # 25 on her Phonics Introduction Page.

Say, "Today we are going to learn the sound *ew*"

Write *ew* in the box on the right-hand side of your page.

Say, "Okay, you write *ew*, too."

Your child writes *ew* in her box.

Say, "*Ew* makes the *oo* sound. Can you say that?"
Your daughter says *oo*.

Look at Lesson 25 in the appendix. Find the words with the *ew* sound.
Say, "*Ew* is used in a lot of words. Here's one, *new.*"

Say, "N," and write *n* on the first line.

Say, "E," and write *e*.

Say, "W, and write *w*.

Say, "New. N-E-W spells *new*. Now it's your turn."

Say, "N."
Your daughter says and writes *n*.

Say, "*E*"
Your daughter says and writes *e*.

Say, "W."
Your daughter says and writes *w*.

Say, "So what does that spell?"
She says, "New!"

Repeat this process with all of the words from Lesson 25. Sometimes there will be more words than lines available on the Phonics Introduction Page. Use the back of the page or copy another page and staple the two together. You may pick and choose words from the list, but try to do as many words as possible, even when you want to pull out your hair! The more examples of a phonics rule your daughter sees and writes, the faster learning can take place. The rule will only become a pattern through example after example.

This process starts off slowly, but by the third or fourth word, your daughter will probably catch on and realize that all of the words are spelled with *ew* and rhyme with one another! They belong to the same *word family*.

Let's continue teaching part two of Lesson 25...

1. Ready- FIND THE PICTURE SENTENCE AND THE PICTURE BOX

Look at Lesson 25 in the **Appendix Part 3 LESSONS**. Find the *picture sentence* for the lesson: *The few knew that the flower grew*. This picture sentence uses a number of the words from the lesson.

Find the *picture box* on the left-hand side of the page.

2. On Your Marks- START TALKING

You say, "Wow! Look at all of these *ew* words! Let's read them together."
You and your daughter read the list of words.

You say, "In the book I found a sentence that uses some of the *ew* words. I am going to read the sentence and write it under this picture box. Then you will do the same thing on your paper."

3. Get Set and Go! (See example on page 186)

You say, "Here's the sentence. *The few knew that the flower grew*."
Say each word of the picture sentence out loud as you write it on the lines underneath the picture box. Repeat the sentence a few times.

Say, "Now *you* write the sentence."
Let your daughter copy the sentence from your paper. Repeat the sentence a few words at a time if necessary.

When your daughter is finished copying the sentence, ask, "What does this sentence say, again?"
She says, "The few knew that the flower grew."
You say, "Fantastic! Can you draw a picture in the box to help yourself remember the sentence?"

Spend a minute or two discussing what ideas you daughter has for the picture. How about a flower? Is the flower growing? Are there people in the picture? How many are a *few*, anyway? In all of my years of teaching and tutoring, I have only come across one child that did not like to color and draw. Most children love art of any kind, and, unfortunately, they aren't able to express themselves through art as often as they should. Creating, drawing and coloring a picture are fun and make a nice break from reading and writing. When drawing, your child is thinking about the meanings of the words she has just read and written. Depending on your daughter's age and time restraints, let her sketch a quick picture in pencil. Save coloring and details for later. What a fun and easy way to redirect her attention to the Phonics Introduction Page outside of formal tutoring.

You now have two, nearly-complete Phonics Introduction Pages (your tutor copy and your daughter's student copy). Put one on the refrigerator next to the sight words and one in the tutoring binder to review next time. Three-hole punch it for easy access.

A few things to remember:

- ✔ Speak slowly and clearly.
- ✔ Say each letter and word out loud as you write it.
- ✔ Repeat the rule, "*ew* makes the *oo* sound," frequently.
- ✔ Pretend that you are forgetful and you need your daughter to repeat the rule for *your* benefit, "Wait! What sound does *ew* make, again? I keep forgetting!" Children will get a kick out of this even if they know you are only pretending to forget.
- ✔ Bring your child's attention back to her Phonics Introduction page as often as possible by asking her questions like, "How many *ew* words do we have?" or "What was the last *ew* word we did?" or "Did we already do *flew*?"
- ✔ Ask your daughter to think of any other *ew* words. When she says, "Dew!" you need to act like she hit the jackpot (she did) and add it to the list with fanfare.

I often leave the last line blank, put a star next to it and say, "If you find an *ew* word, we'll put it here!" The power of suggestion is strong. Students will find *ew* words- or whatever words you are learning- everywhere! Amazing!

Handwriting

This is as good a time as any to discuss handwriting. Some of you look back fondly on the days when penmanship was an actual subject taught in school. You may have beautiful handwriting yourself. I respect your desire for nice and neat handwriting, but keep in mind that the time you spend tutoring your child to reading mastery should not be used for extensive handwriting instruction. I wholeheartedly agree that your daughter's handwriting needs to be neat and legible, and if her writing is sloppy, by all means, have her erase and rewrite. But, please don't make an issue of handwriting. Find some other time to specifically focus on it.

Word Wheels

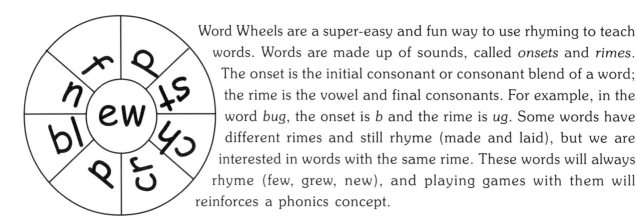

Word Wheels are a super-easy and fun way to use rhyming to teach words. Words are made up of sounds, called *onsets* and *rimes*. The onset is the initial consonant or consonant blend of a word; the rime is the vowel and final consonants. For example, in the word *bug*, the onset is *b* and the rime is *ug*. Some words have different rimes and still rhyme (made and laid), but we are interested in words with the same rime. These words will always rhyme (few, grew, new), and playing games with them will reinforces a phonics concept.

🚩 1. Ready- MAKE COPIES AND FILL IN THE WORD WHEEL

Make copies of the blank word wheel found in **Appendix Part 3 LESSONS**.

Using the words for Lesson 25 found in Words for Word Wheels (also in **Appendix Part Three LESSONS**), follow the directions on the Word Wheel Page. Write the rime in the middle of the wheel, and the onsets on the spokes around it.

2. On Your Marks- START TALKING

Say, "Did you notice that these *ew* words rhyme? You did?!
Let's put them all together on this Word Wheel."

3. Get Set – MODEL

Turn the wheel, aligning onset *d* and rime *ew*.
Say, *"Duh plus ew is dew."*
Turn the wheel to the next onset *f*.
Say *"f* plus *ew* is few."

4. Go! YOUR CHILD LEARNS

Let your daughter try the next onset and rime.

I suggest making a Word Wheel for every lesson, if possible, and keeping it on your jam-packed refrigerator. Challenge your daughter to read all of the words in a certain amount of time, say before the microwave beeps in 20 seconds.

When you move on to a new lesson, put the old Word Wheels in the binder for review.

Cloze Sentences

Cloze sentences are sentences with words missing. Students fill in the blanks with a choice of words. Cloze are revealing: they tell us whether or not a child is able to read a particular sentence, understand the sentence even with some words missing, read the word choices, and chose the word that fits the context and meaning of the sentence.

1. Ready- FIND THE CLOZE SENTENCES

Find the cloze sentences with the other lesson information. Continuing with Lesson 25, you will find the following cloze sentences:
I need a <u>few</u> more dollars. He <u>threw</u> the ball. My shoes are brand <u>new</u>.

2. On Your Marks- START TALKING

Tutor says, "So, we've been looking at these words all week, and I want to see if you can use them in sentences! I am going to write a few sentences."
Write the cloze sentences at the bottom of the Phonics Introduction Page that you have been using all along (use the back of the page if you need more room). Do NOT copy the words that are underlined- leave them blank.

Sample Lesson for Word Wheels

Lesson# Example- aw
aw: draw, straw, awful*, law, awkward*, paw, saw, raw
*these do not follow the onset/rime pattern, but work nonetheless!

(word wheel: center "aw", segments: str, r, l, s, p, ful, kward, p)

Sample Phonics Introduction Page

Lesson #Example- aw
Words: awkward, brawl, draw, straw, hawk, crawl, awful, lawn, dawn, law
Picture Box Sentence: The hawk ate straw on the lawn.
Cloze Sentences: I feel awful that I forgot your birthday. The baby can crawl across the lawn. The argument turned into a brawl.

Phonics Introduction

Lesson # ___ example
Introduction to: **aw**

The hawk ate straw on the lawn.

Words:

awkward	crawl
draw	lawn
brawl	straw
hawk	dawn
awful	law

Cloze Sentences:
I feel <u>awful</u> that I forgot your birthday.
The baby can <u>crawl</u> across the floor.
The argument turned into a <u>brawl</u>.

Write:

I need a_____ more dollars.

He _____ the ball.

My shoes are brand _____.

3. Get Set and Go!

Before you begin, have your daughter copy the sentences, including space for the missing words, onto her Phonics Introduction Page.

> Say, "Let's look at this first sentence. One of the words is missing, so I will have to read it without all of the words. I need a blank more dollars. I wonder what word from our list will fit into the sentence to help it make sense? Let's read the *ew* words from our list."

Read the *ew* words from the Phonics Introduction Page.

> Say, "I need blank more dollars. Which one of those words would fit into this sentence? Let's try the first one, *dew*. I need a *dew* more dollars. Does that make sense? No! What about the next one? I need a *new* more dollars? No way! How about I need a *few* more dollars? I agree! That makes sense! Let's write *few* on the line. Great!"

Repeat with all of the sentences. You want to get to the point where your daughter is completing the cloze sentences with little or no help from you.

Putting It All Together

Some phonics concepts will be relatively easy for your daughter; others will be more challenging. Spend as long on each lesson as your daughter needs. Don't rush. You have the luxury of time; use it.

Here is an easy three day phonics plan:

> Day 1:
> Introduce a new lesson with a Phonics Introduction Page.
> Play a quick game of Tic-Tac-Toe with the new words.

Make a set of phonics flash cards.

Day 2:
Review Phonics Introduction Page.
Play Memory with flash cards.
Complete a Word Wheel.

Day 3:
Review Phonics Introduction Page
Complete Cloze Sentences

Remember there are dozens of games, tips, ideas, books and lessons for teaching phonics! Use the ones here and the information in the **Appendix Part 3 LESSONS** to get you started. Feel free to mix sight words and phonics when playing games like Memory and Tic-Tac-Toe. Mix words from different phonics lessons (Lesson 25 and Lesson 99, for example). Review, review, review!

CHAPTER *12*

HOW TO TEACH FLUENCY

Fluency, as your remember from **Chapter 2 How Children Learn to Read,** measures reading speed and accuracy. Fluency has become a huge subject. I once attended an all-day fluency training workshop. The speaker *began* the training by apologizing for running out of time! He understood that we could spend that entire day and the months following discussing fluency, and only have gotten started. Studies are being conducted, books are being written, and educators are constantly debating the best way to teach our children how to read well and with understanding. Tutor Your Child to Reading Success discusses fluency last because children must be able to recognize sight words and decode phonics first.

Fluent readers display three reading traits: accuracy (few, if any, reading errors), automaticity (instant word recognition) and *prosody* (expression and intonation). Some children need instruction in just one or two of these areas, while others need tutoring in all three. You have been addressing the accuracy component by making certain that your son recognizes sight words and can decode other words. By reviewing and retesting the words in each lesson until mastery, your son will soon have automaticity. Let's talk about the last component, prosody.

Prosody is reading with meaning and expression, emphasizing the right words, stopping at periods, pausing at commas, exclaiming at exclamation points, and raising one's voice when asking a question. A prosodic reader reads with animation and expression because he understands and is engaged in what he is reading. The flip side of that coin is, he understands what he is reading *because* he reads with animation and expression. It's the chicken-egg debate.

Two things must occur for your son to become a prosodic reader: one, he must be shown how to do it; two, he must practice doing it correctly.

If we want children to read with expression, we must provide an example. We show our children how to work hard, make an omelet, throw a curve ball, wash the dishes, treat friends- and, now, how to read fluently. When our children are very young, it seems natural to sit down and read with them. But, it's important when they are older, as well, especially if we are trying to help them become fluent readers. While you are tutoring your child to reading success, you will return to the days when you and your child sat down and read together. It is my sincerest wish that you will continue to read together even when your son is a reading wizard and formal tutoring has ended!

The second requirement for helping your son become an expressive reader is practice. Despite what we have been told, practice does not make perfect: *correct* practice makes perfect. Doing a task incorrectly over and over again only makes you good at doing it incorrectly. In order for your son to become a fluent reader, he must practice reading correctly.

So, you are going to show him how to read fluently, then you are going to listen to him read fluently. Over and over again.

But wait, there aren't any fluency lessons in this book! You won't find any stories or paragraphs in the **Appendix Part 3 LESSONS** (trust me). You must be wondering *what am I going to use to help my son become a fluent reader?*

You could purchase a fluency program. Many of these programs offer training classes where you buy materials (short lessons and audiotapes, usually) to use with students. Some of these programs are expensive, some are not. Some are quite good, others leave a lot to be desired. When I tutored students once a week, I did, in fact, use one of these programs for fluency practice because the lessons could be completed during one tutoring session.

You, lucky parent, are in a much, much better position! You can tutor your child *every day!* What an opportunity! You don't have to settle for reading leveled paragraphs. You can sell your child on the wonders of real *books*. Please, please, please introduce your son to some fabulous literature!

People are quite naturally shocked to learn that many children are not reading books in school. Oh, students go to the library and check out books, but they are left to read them *on their own*. Right. I want to see children really reading a book with the teacher, having class discussions, learning about plot development and characterization. Sadly, this is happening less and less. Students are given basal readers with short stories and excerpts from novels. They start a new story on Monday, get tested on Friday, and the whole thing starts over next week. Our children have no idea how it feels to get lost in a novel or spend a week talking about symbolism or getting to really know a character.

It's up to you. Show your son that reading is a worthwhile activity because there are some fantastic books out there just waiting for him. Introduce him to hilarious, sad, scary, gross, unbelievable books with silly, unforgettable, complicated, strange, lovely, characters in faraway, close-to-home, amazing places! If your can turn your son on to the joys of reading, you will have an eager, willing student on your hands. Your son will want to read if he thinks there is something out there to read that is as interesting as TV and video games.

It is a cinch to sell a child on reading. What is being written these days is phenomenal, and you can probably find most of the books you loved as a child.

There has always been outstanding children's literature, but there is so much more of it being published now. Go into the children's section of any bookstore and be prepared to be astounded by the quality, quantity and variety of literature available. I believe that the biggest reason for the new interest in children's literature is money. With the success of the Harry Potter series, the world realized that a fortune could be made writing for people who, supposedly, have no cash of their own.

Another reason for the interest in children's literature is the Nostalgia Factor. From bean bag chairs to Davy Crockett raccoon hats, we all want to return to the good ole days of our happy and carefree youth. Everything retro is in style- including the children's books of yesterday. It makes sense. Is there a better way to revisit your childhood than opening a book you loved as a child?

Let's talk about all of the places that parents can find superb children's literature.

Where to Find Books for Your Child

TV

That's right- TV. One of the best places to find literature for your child is that big, black hole sitting in the living room. You thought that you were pretty cool with that Partridge Family lunch box? Please! These days popular children's TV shows and their stars are mass marketed *beyond belief*. If a television show is even mildly popular, they'll create an entire world around it: movies, video games, toys, fast food giveaways, prizes, even clothing! But, the one piece of the mass marketing pie that parents should relish is a new literary genre that I call the TV Book.

Remember when the book came before the movie? Things have changed.

The book, or book series, now *follows* the movie or the TV show. Don't roll your eyes! I think this is a great development. Some teachers and parents only want children to read *real* literature written by *serious* authors, but, remember, the goal is to get kids reading. In the beginning, it might be a whole lot easier to get your child to pick up a book based on his favorite TV show than a classic he has never heard of and think will bore him senseless. If your son loves a book based on a TV show, let him read it! Ask him which he thinks is better, the book or the TV show. Before you know it, you'll be discussing something other than cleaning his room or eating his vegetables. You will have plenty of opportunities to get him reading the classics.

Bookstores

Of course, you can find children's literature in bookstores (duh), but did you know that many bookstores have their own clubs, similar to airlines' frequent flier miles? The more books you buy, the more books you can get free. This might not seem like such a big deal now, but when your child soon becomes a voracious reader, you'll be glad to save a few dollars.

Some of the large bookstore chains feel overwhelming- there are so many books! My daughter has wandered up and down the aisles in the children's section many times unable to find anything. I've found that asking the people that work there for help can be a great starting point. They can tell you what books are flying off the shelves, which books should be flying off the shelves, which book just received an important award, all sorts of information.

The great thing about smaller, local book stores is that once they get to know you, a beautiful literary relationship can develop. They'll tell you about upcoming sales or call you when a book has come in by your favorite author. Wouldn't you love for your child to be a bookstore *regular*?

Book Clubs through School

Many parents are familiar with the school book clubs. Basically, these clubs are direct-sales companies, which is why their prices are so affordable. Students are given an order form that includes a brief synopsis of grade-level books. Students choose books (sometimes toys, games and software) and return the order form and money to the teacher. The teacher sends in the classroom order form, and is then driven crazy by students asking, "Is the book order in yet?" every day for the next three weeks. While I will never stop going to bookstores because I love the experience of seeing, smelling and browsing, book clubs are a good deal. The prices are reasonable, and the classroom earns points for books purchased. The points can be redeemed for free books and supplies. Not only will you help your child build a personal library, you will be helping a teacher build a classroom library.

If your child has never mentioned or brought home a book order, ask about it. He might not have brought the order form home because he didn't plan on ordering. Tell him that you read about these book clubs, and *you* want to see an order form. Look through it and tell him to chose a book (not a toy) or you will find something for him. Don't listen to any protests. Students always light up and smile when the teacher hands them their book order.

If your child's teacher isn't doing book orders, find out if another teacher will let you place an order with her class. I did this for a student once, and she ordered $64! The next year the teacher began doing book orders.

School Book Fairs

Most schools participate in book fairs. These book fairs are fund-raisers for the school and are sponsored by the same companies that sell books in book clubs. Imagine that. The nice thing about book fairs is that students are able to hold the books in their hands before choosing and can take the books home immediately.

Book Clubs

These clubs have been around forever, and you can find them for music and movies as well as books. They usually grab your attention by offering an unbelievable introductory prize like 6 books for $0.99. By signing up, you agree to purchase a certain number of books at the club's regular prices during the next year. In addition, each month they will offer you a deal on a special book- that month's selection. You want to be careful to quickly send back the form stating whether or not you want that month's selection. If they don't hear from you, or if they hear from you too late, you will find the book in your mailbox. You will either have to pay for it or deal with the hassle of a return. Despite these hassles, book clubs are convenient, competitive, and great ways to earn free books.

Garage Sales

I have found many of my children's books at garage sales, tag sales, flea markets and white elephant sales. Talk about incredible bargains! Most people aren't trying to get rich off of their old books, they just don't want to throw them away. Be sure to flip through and check the condition of each book before buying it. Even $1.00 is too much to pay for <u>Huckleberry Finn</u> if the pages are missing or sticky with juice. A garage sale is also a great way to sell your old books.

Book Swap

There are books that you and your children will never want to sell or give away. On the other hand, there will be dozens of books that your children no longer read and could not care less about. Get together with some of their friends and have a book swap. Each child brings 5 or 10 books in good condition that they no longer read. The books are put into one pile, and kids take turns picking 5 or 10 new books. Everybody goes home with new books, and it didn't cost a dime!

Library

You may find it odd that I didn't mention the library first. I have a love-hate relationship with the library. This is my own, weird personal issue. I fully believe that our public library system is one of our country's greatest achievements. Millions of books to read for free! Thanks to the public library, there is nothing we can't learn, nothing we can't teach our children and no story that can't be shared. It's a fabulous thing. My problem is that I like buying books. I don't mind sharing, loaning, even giving away my books. But, when I have them, I like to know that they are mine. Returning a book to the library feels a little bit like having a test at the end of every chapter- it takes the fun out of reading. But, that's just me. My children don't even know how I feel about the library. They think I love it because I take them there all of the time.

How to Choose Books for Your Child

You know *where* to find books, but before we discuss *which* books to choose for your children, I'd like to give you one piece of advice: READ THE BOOK BEFORE YOU READ IT WITH YOUR CHIILD! I learned this lesson the hard way. After reading an excerpt of a story in the basal reader, I decided to find the entire book and read it to my fourth grade class. We had read part of the book in class, so I figured that the rest would be fine. Big mistake! I was unprepared when we came across inappropriate language in the book not found in the excerpt. I made the difficult and unpopular decision of quitting a book in the middle.

Memory

Think back to your own childhood. Were there any books you *especially* loved? It is easy to get your child excited about a book that has personal meaning and good memories for you. If you don't remember any books, perhaps a parent, sibling or an relative remembers a book you loved as a child. I don't know if my son will recall <u>Is Your Mama A Llama?</u> as a grown man, but I will certainly never forget reading it to him night after night.

Word of Mouth

Ask your friends what books their children are reading. Ask your child's teacher what books he would like your child to read. Ask the librarian which books are checked out the most.

Best Sellers and Award Winners

There used to be a time, not so long ago, when the literati snubbed their noses at children's literature. Those days are over. Children's literature is big business, with as much recognition, attention and prestige as adult literature. Newspapers, bookstores and online booksellers are more than happy to tell you which children's books are winning awards and selling like hotcakes.

There are plenty of people ready to tell you which books to buy. Some people love good children's literature, and honestly want to share and recommend it. Others are solely interested in taking your hard-earned money. Be sure to take advice from book lovers. Look in **Appendix Part 3 LESSONS** for organizations and websites to help you choose the right books for your child.

My Book Club

How about a little shameless self-promotion? Go to my website, www.NatomasTutoring.com, for book reviews and recommendations written by children and teachers.

Reading Difficulty

Another consideration in choosing books for your child is reading difficulty. While we do not want a child to make a big deal out of grade-level, it is still important to consider this information when selecting books for fluency practice. The books you and your son read together should be at his *instructional level (he is able to read 90% - 95% of the words found in the book correctly)*. If a book is at his **frustration level** (he can read less than 90% of the words), your son will spend most of his time trying to decode words and not working on fluency or comprehension.

A quick way to find out if a book is at your son's instructional level is to open it up anywhere and ask him to read a paragraph. If he struggles over most of the words, you know the book is too difficult. If he is able to read most of the words, even slowly, the book is probably a good one for fluency practice. If he breezes through the book, consider buying it for his *independent* reading (more than 95% of the words read correctly).

Finally, don't forget *age appropriateness*. Your 5th grader may read at a 3rd grade level (for the time being), but that does *not* mean he wants to read a 3rd grade book. Some children don't mind reading books that have been written for younger readers; other children would rather jump out a window than do so. The best books continue to delight readers of all ages and grade levels. One of my all-time favorite books, <u>Sarah, Plain and Tall</u> by Patricia Mac Lachlan, is usually referred to as a 4th grade book. However, all of my 4th, 5th and 6th graders enjoyed reading it. A good story is a good story. Once again, parent, you are trying to strike a balance. You don't want to bore or demoralize your child, but at the same time, he needs to practice reading at his instructional level! Explain that as his reading improves, so will the selection.

In the **Appendix Part Three LESSONS**, you will find information to help you choose books based on subject and reading-level.

Now let's talk about how to practice fluency with your child.

🏳 *1. Ready-* CHOOSE LENGTH AND DISCUSSION QUESTIONS

You have chosen a book for fluency practice. It will make your life much easier if both you and your son have a copy of the book. This is especially true with older (4th grade and up) children who are used to holding reading material in their own hands and not reading with someone looking over their shoulder. One of the benefits of going to the library is that you can usually find two copies of a book.

Before reading with your child, you have two quick chores: pick a stopping point and think of some discussion questions.

You want about a minutes' worth of reading, usually one or two paragraphs at the instruction level. This is a good length: not too long, not too short. Your child can quickly learn the words he does not know, and he will be able to practice reading on his own. You will soon learn to gauge the amount.

A large part of fluency is comprehension. By asking discussion questions and listening to your son's answers, you will quickly know whether or not your son has understood what he has read. Read the paragraphs and jot some quick notes about which words, ideas, concepts and questions you will discuss with your son. There are study guides for many children's books, but I tend to think that discussing the 5 Ws and 1H- who, what, when, where, why, and how- is best.

Once again, I recommend that the tutor sits on the left, student on the right.

2. On Your Marks- START TALKING

Before reading a passage, you will want to do the following:
- ✔ Review punctuation and remind him of its purpose.
- ✔ Point out any difficult words that you think your child might have trouble with, especially proper nouns like names and places and words critical to understanding the passage.

You say, "We've been practicing sight words, and, my goodness, you are learning so many of them! And, what a good job you are doing with phonics, too! I am so proud of you! But, the whole point of learning all of those words is to be able to read them when you see them, right? I am so excited that we found this great book (read the title), aren't you? Before we start reading, though, I want you to ask you a couple of things. What is this thing? That's right, a period! What do you do when you see a period? You stop reading. Okay, what is this thing? A comma. And what do we do when we see commas? We pause or slow down, that's right! Now, these commas and periods are very important. The author puts them there so we can read the words the right way and understand what is going on. If there weren't any periods or commas, the sentences would just run on and on, and we wouldn't understand anything! Here are a few words from the story that you might not know."

Tutor gives correct pronunciation and discusses meaning of no more than four or five important words.

3. Go! YOUR CHILD READS

Say, "Let's get started. Take your time."

Your child reads the passage. Take quick notes about misread words, punctuation issues, reading speed and expression.

4. Go! YOU MODEL READING

You say, 'Good job! You knew a lot of those words, didn't you? Now I want you to listen to me read it. I am going to read like I am on stage reading in front of an audience! I am going to exaggerate because I want you to get an idea of how to read with a lot of expression. There's something else. You have to follow along while I read, no looking out of the window! Stay with me while I'm reading. Your eyes should see the word and your ears should hear the word as it is coming out of my mouth. This way it will get into your brain quickly, and you'll be a fast reader, too!"

Read the passage with exaggerated expression, intonation, and feeling. Your reading is over-the-top because you want your son to really understand what fluent reading sounds like. Older children will probably be mortified and embarrassed beyond belief by your performance. But, guess what? Everything you do embarrasses them, and it will for years! Let them laugh; at least they will know fluent reading when they hear it.

5. Go! DISCUSS THE READING

After you have both read the passage once, stop and talk about it. What is this story about? Who are the characters? When is it taking place? What happened, and what do you think is going to happen next? Ask enough questions so that you know whether or not your son understands the main points of the story. If you realize that he has not understood something, return to the passage and read it again!

6. Go! YOU AND YOUR CHILD READ

> Say, "Okay, now I want us to read it together. Ready?"
> You and your child read the passage together, in unison.

The first few times, most children will let you do all the talking. They might say a word here and there. Be ready for this. Stop and say, "Hey! What's going on here? You're letting me do all of the work! We're supposed to read together! I need to hear your voice!" Make a joke out of it, but don't let it continue.

7. Go! YOUR CHILD READS

> You say, "That wasn't so bad, was it? We sounded pretty good! Now, I want you to read the passage one last time by yourself."
> Student reads the passage.

Your son has only read and/or heard the text read three times, but he will be able to read it much better. His word recognition skills and his expression will have improved in only a few minutes. Some people would tell you to have your son read the passage over and over again until he can read it fast and with no mistakes. I strongly disagree. You are not only practicing fluency, you are trying to sell your child on reading. Reading is an enjoyable activity, remember? If you make him read the same passage over and over again, your son will find reading boring and come to resent the whole process. Don't work against yourself. Four times is enough.

> Say, "Wow! Did you hear how much faster and smoother you sounded that time? You did a fantastic job, but I think that is enough for today. You can hold onto the book and practice this passage later if you want." Prepare to be blown away when your son says, "I don't want to stop! Can we keep going?"

The next time you and your son practice fluency, have him reread the last passage as a quick review and to get him excited about reading the next passage.

The process is always the same:

He reads.
You read.
You both read.
He reads.

You will find that as your son's reading improves, the length of passages increases. In the beginning, your passages might only be a few short paragraphs. Next thing you know, a passage is a page, then two pages, then three. One day, he'll be reading entire books on his own, and you'll watch in wonder.

Oh, the excitement!

	Fluent Reader	*Mostly Fluent*	*Somewhat Fluent*	*Non-Fluent*
Accuracy	98%-100% (misses 0-2 words out of 100)	95%-100% (misses 0-5 words out of 100)	90% (misses 10 out of 100 words)	less than 90% (misses more than 10 out of 100 words)
Pays Attention to Punctuation	yes (stops at periods, pauses at commas, raises voice for question marks, shows surprise at exclamation points)	usually	no	no
Expression	very expressive (voice rises and falls, stresses correct words)	some expression	little or no expression	no expression-monotonic
Corrects Mistakes	yes	usually	sometimes	no
Smoothness	very smooth-seamless reading	smooth-few breaks, some choppiness, often reads in 3-word phrases	choppy-starts, stops, repeats words, sounds out words	very choppy
Comprehension	good- understands all of text	fair-understands most	limited- understands little	none
Volume	appropriate- easy to hear	generally appropriate	mostly quiet	usually quiet- hard to hear
Pace/ Speed	consistently conversational	slow and fast	slow	slow, laborious

Table 5 - This table shows that speed is not the only consideration in determining fluency. For example, a child can read with 100% accuracy (know all of the words right), but if she pays no attention to punctuation, reads with no expression, and does not correct her mistakes, she is not a fluent reader.

How Many CORRECT Words Per Minute (CWPM) Should My Child Be Reading?

Grade:		Beginning	Middle	End
2nd	50%	53	70	94
	75%	82	98	124
3rd	50%	79	88	114
	75%	107	118	142
4th	50%	99	108	118
	75%	125	130	143
5th	50%	105	114	128
	75%	126	137	151
6th	50%	125	138	150
	75%	145	155	170

What does it mean?

50%- If your child is reading at this level, it means that he or she is reading at grade level.

75%- A student reading at this level is considered a good reader.

Contents

See ***Chapter 6 How to Give Sight Word Assessments*** and
Chapter 10 How to Teach Sight Word Lessons

100 MOST COMMON SIGHT WORDS (S100)

1. the
2. of
3. and
4. a
5. to
6. in
7. is
8. you
9. that
10. it
11. he
12. for
13. was
14. on
15. are
16. as
17. with
18. his
19. they
20. at
21. be
22. this
23. from
24. I
25. have
26. or
27. by
28. one
29. had
30. not
31. but
32. what
33. all
34. were

35. when
36. we
37. there
38. can
39. an
40. your
41. which
42. their
43. said
44. if
45. do
46. will
47. each
48. about
49. how
50. up
51. out
52. them
53. then
54. she
55. many
56. some
57. so
58. these
59. would
60. other
61. into
62. has
63. more
64. her
65. two
66. like
67. him

68. see
69. time
70. could
71. no
72. make
73. than
74. first
75. been
76. its
77. who
78. now
79. people
80. my
81. made
82. over
83. did
84. down
85. only
86. way
87. find
88. use
89. may
90. water
91. long
92. little
93. very
94. after
95. words
96. called
97. just
98. where
99. most
100. know

See *Chapter 6 How to Give Sight Word Assessments* and
Chapter 10 How to Teach Sight Word Lessons

Sight Words- Step 1 (Early 1ˢᵗ Grade) (SE1)

1. would
2. make
3. like
4. him
5. into
6. time
7. has
8. look
9. more
10. write
11. other
12. about
13. out
14. many
15. then
16. them
17. these
18. so
19. some
20. her
21. use
22. an
23. each
24. which
25. do
26. how

27. their
28. if
29. will
30. up
31. not
32. what
33. all
34. were
35. we
36. when
37. your
38. can
39. said
40. there
41. be
42. this
43. have
44. from
45. or
46. one
47. had
48. by
49. word
50. but
51. he
52. was
53. for

54. on
55. are
56. as
57. with
58. his
59. they
60. I
61. the
62. of
63. and
64. a
65. to
66. in
67. is
68. you
69. that
70. it

See *Chapter 6 How to Give Sight Word Assessments* and
Chapter 10 How to Teach Sight Word Lessons

SIGHT WORDS- STEP 1 (MIDDLE AND LATE 1ST GRADE) (SML1)

1. go
2. see
3. number
4. no
5. way
6. could
7. people
8. my
9. than
10. first
11. most
12. very
13. after
14. thing
15. our
16. just
17. name
18. sentence
19. good
20. man
21. only
22. little
23. work
24. know
25. place
26. year
27. live
28. me
29. back
30. give
31. day
32. did
33. get
34. made
35. may
36. part

37. over
38. new
39. sound
40. take
41. water
42. been
43. call
44. who
45. oil
46. its
47. now
48. find
49. long
50. down
51. off
52. again
53. land
54. men
55. went
56. spell
57. need
58. ask
59. kind
60. picture
61. home
62. more
63. why
64. different
65. try
66. read
67. show
68. such
69. also
70. form
71. around
72. well

73. want
74. end
75. set
76. large
77. even
78. small
79. turn
80. another
81. put
82. three
83. must
84. even
85. because
86. big
87. before
88. follow
89. too
90. boy
91. old
92. great
93. same
94. where
95. any
96. came
97. line
99. tell
100. think
101. much
102. man
103. through
104. mean
105. right
106. say
107. help

See *Chapter 6 How to Give Sight Word Assessments* and
Chapter 10 How to Teach Sight Word Lessons

SIGHT WORDS- STEP 1 (2ND GRADE) (S2)

1. study
2. still
3. learn
4. should
5. America
6. world
7. high
8. every
9. near
10. add
11. air
12. away
13. animal
14. house
15. point
16. page
17. letter
18. mother
19. answer
20. found
21. move
22. try
23. kind
24. hand

25. picture
26. again
27. change
28. off
29. play
30. spell

See *Chapter 6 How to Give Sight Word Assessments* and
Chapter 10 How to Teach Sight Word Lessons

SIGHT WORDS- STEP 2 (3ʳᵈ & 4ᵗʰ GRADES) (S34)

1. tree	30. both	59. without
2. never	31. paper	60. second
3. start	32. together	61. almost
4. city	33. got	62. let
5. earth	34. group	63. above
6. eye	35. often	64. girl
7. light	36. run	65. sometimes
8. thought	37. important	66. mountain
9. head	38. until	67. cut
10. under	39. children	68. young
11. story	40. side	69. talk
12. saw	41. feet	70. soon
13. left	42. car	71. late
14. don't	43. mile	72. miss
15. few	44. night	73. idea
16. while	45. walk	74. enough
17. along	46. white	75. eat
18. might	47. sea	76. face
19. chose	48. began	77. watch
20. something	49. grow	78. far
21. seem	50. took	79. Indian
22. next	51. river	80. really
23. hard	52. four	81. list
24. open	53. carry	82. song
25. example	54. state	83. being
26. begin	55. once	84. leave
27. life	56. book	85. family
28. always	57. hear	86. its
29. those	58. stop	

See **Chapter 6 How to Give Sight Word Assessments** and
Chapter 10 How to Teach Sight Word Lessons

SIGHT WORDS
COLORS, MONTHS, NUMBERS, DAYS OF THE WEEK (S)

1. red
2. blue
3. yellow
4. green
5. purple
6. orange
7. brown
8. black
9. gray
10. white
11. one
12. two
13. three
14. four
15. five
16. six
17. seven
18. eight
19. nine
20. ten
21. eleven
22. twelve
23. thirteen
24. fourteen
25. fifteen
26. sixteen
27. seventeen
28. eighteen
29. nineteen
30. twenty
31. thirty
32. forty
33. fifty
34. sixty
35. seventy
36. eighty
37. ninety
38. hundred
39. thousand
40. million
41. January
42. February
43. March
44. April
45. May
46. June
47. July
48. August
49. September
50. October
51. November
52. December
53. Monday
54. Tuesday
55. Wednesday
56. Thursday
57. Friday
58. Saturday
59. Sunday

Blank Flash Cards

FAVORITE SIGHT WORD WEBSITES

http: //www.DiscoverySchool.com/puzzles

This is a great site for a lot of reasons, but one of its best features is its FREE puzzle maker. Use newly-learned sight words (or any words you choose, for that matter) to create puzzles that will delight your child.

http: //www.literaryconnections.com/SightWordPractice

More super sight word games than you will ever need! Go home and check out the other sections of this website, particularly Especially for Reading Teachers. This website can keep you busy for a lifetime with so many interesting articles about literacy!

http: //www.teachersnet.com/ lessons

See Lesson #485 Activities to Reinforce and Teach Sight Words

This lesson contains some of my all-time favorite sight word games like TicTacToe, as well as others. Most of the lessons are for teachers to use in a classroom, but can easily be modified for one learner.

See Lesson # 1224 Dolch Sight Word Games

This lesson contains a great 675-word story than contains all of the 220 Dolch Basic Sight Words. This is a super assessment. Scroll down after the story to find sight word teaching ideas from parents and teachers.

See ***Chapter 11 How to Teach Phonics Lessons***

STEP 1 PHONICS LESSONS (P1)

Lesson #1- short a *
Words: bag, am, and, can, had, black, grab, cat, shall, sang, thank
Picture Box Sentence: The man had a black bag.
Cloze Sentences: I <u>am</u> sad. We <u>sang</u> a song. <u>Thank</u> you very much!

Lesson #2- short e*
Words: beg, red, ten, let, tell, end, hen, never, dress, chest
Picture Box Sentence: The bell fell on his chest.
Cloze Sentences: My brother is <u>ten</u>. The <u>hen</u> lays eggs. Do you like my new <u>dress</u>?

Lesson #3- short i*
Words: big, inch, fill, hid, think, swim, thick, kid, print, dish
Picture Box Sentence: He will drink the big glass of milk.
Cloze Sentences: We <u>hid</u> in the closet. Can you <u>swim</u>? The food is in the <u>dish</u>.

Lesson #4- short o
Words: bog, got, fox, dog, not, off, top, doll, cross, block, strong
Picture Box Sentence: The dog wore a costume.
Cloze Sentences: The <u>fox</u> was sly. The glass fell <u>off</u> the table. Look both ways before you <u>cross</u> the street.

Lesson #5- short u
Words: bug, up, us, fun, bus, sun, run, truck, drum, crush
Picture Box Sentence: The summer sun was yellow and red.
Cloze Sentences: The <u>bug</u> flew in the door. She can <u>run</u> fast. The <u>drum</u> is loud.

Lesson #6- long e
Words: he, she, we, be, me
Picture Box Sentence: We are best friends.
Cloze Sentences: <u>He</u> is a boy. <u>She</u> is a girl. <u>We</u> are a family.

Lesson #7- long o*
Words: so, go, no, old, cold, mold, fold
Picture Box Sentence: I am so cold in the snow!
Cloze Sentences: The man is <u>old</u>. The <u>mold</u> is green and stinky. Let's <u>fold</u> the clothes.

---

* see page 239 Word for Word Wheels

Lesson #8- a/ final e*
Words: name, gave, take, made, late, wave, rake, page, sale, shape, plane, safe, chase
Picture Box Sentence: I do not like the taste of cake.
Cloze Sentences: Her <u>name</u> is Molly. The <u>wave</u> hit the beach. The <u>shape</u> is a square.

Lesson #9- e/ final e
Words: here, these, eve
Picture Box Sentence: These are big cats!
Cloze Sentences: <u>Here</u> it is. The night before is called <u>eve</u>. <u>These</u> pickles are sour.

Lesson #10- i/ final e*
Words: five, nine, ride, bike, time, white, wife, smile, wise, size, wire, mile
Picture Box Sentence: I like to ride my white bike one mile.
Cloze Sentences: The <u>wire</u> is hot. She is <u>nine</u> years old. What <u>time</u> is it now?

Lesson #11- o/ final e*
Words: home, close, bone, rope, stole, wrote, nose, woke, rode, chose
Picture Box Sentence: Those kids stole the money.
Cloze Sentences: We <u>woke</u> up and left. My <u>nose</u> itches. The dog ate the <u>bone</u>.

Lesson #12- u/ final e
Words: blue, true, include, rule, mule, cute, cube
Picture Box Sentence: The blue cube was huge.
Cloze Sentences: A <u>mule</u> looks like a horse. The sky is <u>blue</u>. The baby is <u>cute</u>.

Lesson #13- ay*
Words: day, stay, away, gray, pay, today, always, maybe, crayon, birthday
Picture Box Sentence: Today is my birthday! Hooray!
Cloze Sentences: The <u>crayon</u> is called blue-green. Mom said <u>maybe</u> we can go to the park. Stay <u>away</u> from the skunk!

Lesson #14- ai*
Words: rain, tail, bait, maid, claim, chain, train, fail, rail
Picture Box Sentence: The chain hung from the rail on the train.
Cloze Sentences: The dog wagged its <u>tail</u>. The <u>maid</u> cleaned the house. The fish ate the <u>bait</u>.

Lesson #15- ee*
Words: see, feel, feet, need, week, sleep, street, seen, teeth, heel, free
Picture Box Sentence: I could feel the bug on my cheek.
Cloze Sentences: He needs to brush his <u>teeth</u>. Cars drive on the <u>street</u>. My <u>feet</u> stink!

Lesson #16- *ie*
Words: lie, tie, pie, tied, cried, believe
Picture Box Sentence: We made a pie with green apples.
Cloze Sentences: The baby <u>cried</u> all night. I will not tell a <u>lie</u>. He <u>tied</u> his shoes.

Lesson #17- *oa**
Words: road, toad, load, goat, boat, coat, float, soak
Picture Box Sentence: The goat sat on the toad.
Cloze Sentences: We drove on the country <u>road</u>. My <u>coat</u> is warm. Can you <u>float</u> on your back?

Lesson #18- *ea**
Words: ear, leave, clean, easy, each, east, seat, leaf, team, weak, please, meal, lead, cheap, season, peace
Picture Box Sentence: We scream for ice cream!
Cloze Sentences: My favorite <u>season</u> is summer. The <u>leaf</u> fell off the tree. That test was so <u>easy</u>!

Lesson #19- *ou**
Words: out, our, house, round, ground, found, cloud, loud, mountain, mouth, amount
Picture Box Sentence: Our house is round and big.
Cloze Sentences: My teeth are in my <u>mouth</u>. There is snow on the <u>mountain</u>. I <u>found</u> a penny.

Lesson #20- *ow**
Words: now, down, owl, how, cow, brown, flower, crowd, shower, chow, town
Picture Box Sentence: The clown had a brown flower.
Cloze Sentences: The <u>owl</u> hoots at night. There was a <u>crowd</u> at the mall. A <u>cow</u> makes milk.

Lesson #21- *ow = long o**
Words: low, snow, grow, window, tomorrow, pillow, arrow, fellow, own, thrown
Picture Box Sentence: I know how to blow out the candles.
Cloze Sentences: The <u>arrow</u> hit the target. Put your head on the <u>pillow</u>. Look out of the <u>window</u>.

Lesson #22- *oo**
Words: too, soon, food, room, school, tooth, root, choose, goose, tool
Picture Box Sentence: The balloon is red, white and blue.
Cloze Sentences: The <u>food</u> is on the plate. The tree has thick <u>roots</u>. I love my <u>school</u>!

Lesson #23- oy*
Words: boy, toy, joy, enjoy
Picture Box Sentence: I enjoy my new toys.
Cloze Sentences: I <u>enjoy</u> the game. She has a room full of <u>toys</u>. That <u>boy</u> is my brother.

Lesson #24- oi
Words: coin, join, boil, noise, point, voice
Picture Box Sentence: Join my voice and make some noise!
Cloze Sentences: There is a <u>coin</u> in my pocket. The water will <u>boil</u>. It is rude to <u>point</u>.

Lesson #25- ew*
Words: dew, new, blew, knew, drew, grew, flew, threw, few
Picture Box Sentence: The bird grew big and flew away.
Cloze Sentences: I only have a <u>few</u> minutes. I <u>knew</u> the answer. She <u>blew</u> out the candle.

Lesson #26- ar*
Words: car, dark, hard, arm, art, bark, yard, sharp, apart, army, farther
Picture Box Sentence: The stars shined in the dark sky.
Cloze Sentences: My pencil is <u>sharp</u>. The bug crawled on my <u>arm</u>. The dog is in the <u>yard</u>.

Lesson #27- or
Words: short, fork, worn, corner, sport, storm, mirror, born, motor, visitor, cord
Picture Box Sentence: The short horse ran in the storm.
Cloze Sentences: I was <u>born</u> in February. Look at yourself in the <u>mirror</u>. She lives around the <u>corner</u>.

Lesson #28- ir
Words: first, girl, bird, dirt, third, sir, stir, thirsty, skirt
Picture Box Sentence: The bird sat on the girl and drank a soda.
Cloze Sentences: The cook <u>stirs</u> the pot. The <u>first</u> day of school is fun. I drink water because I am <u>thirsty</u>.

Lesson #29- ur
Words: turn, burn, hurt, during, hurry, further, return, curtain
Picture Box Sentence: The curtain blows in the wind.
Cloze Sentences: She fell down and <u>hurt</u> herself. <u>Hurry</u> up, we are going to be late! The fire will <u>burn</u> you.

Lesson #30- er
Words: mother, together, ever, person, number, later, reader, under, perhaps, perfect,
Picture Box Sentence: The ring was silver.
Cloze Sentences: My <u>mother</u> loves me. Seven is my favorite <u>number</u>. The bug is <u>under</u> the rock.

Lesson #31- ch
Words: chip, church, chant, chap, check, chess, cheek, chow, chew, chicken, chirp, chop, chest, cheese
Picture Box Sentence: The chicken chews the cheese .
Cloze Sentences: Do you know how to play <u>chess</u>? There is a small <u>chip</u> in the mirror. The <u>church</u> was quite.

Lesson #32- sh
Words: shack, shadow, sham, shaft, shame, shape, shark, shave, she, shawl, shed, sheep, shop, shirt, shoe, show, shy
Picture Box Sentence: The shark shaves his beard in the shed.
Cloze Sentences: My new <u>shirt</u> is blue and yellow. The woman was cold an put on a <u>shawl</u>. The dog chased its <u>shadow</u>.

Lesson #33- th
Words: than, that, thank, theft, them, then, thick, thin, thorn, thud, thus, throne, thunder
Picture Box Sentence: The thunder was louder than usual.
Cloze Sentences: The flower had a <u>thorn</u> on the stem. The book fell with a <u>thud</u>. <u>Thank</u> you very much.

Lesson #34- wh
Words: whack, wham, wheat, whiff, whim, whimper, whine, whip, whale, whiz, whirl, whisk
Picture Box Sentence: The wheat grew ten feet tall.
Cloze Sentences: The <u>whale</u> is gray. Seeing the whip made the dog <u>whimper</u>. My dad does not like to hear my brother <u>whine</u>.

Lesson #35 –ck*
Words: sack, black, attack, whack, piggyback, check, peck, neck, lick, block, sock, cluck, snuck, o'clock
Picture Box Sentence: There was a car wreck at the race track.
Cloze Sentences: The party is at two <u>o'clock</u>. I <u>lick</u> my lips. My sister gave me <u>piggyback</u> ride.

Lesson #36 –ng*
Words: bang, sang, ring, king, along, earring, song, rung, clung, anything,
Picture Box Sentence: We sang a song at camp.
Cloze Sentences: I put the <u>earring</u> in my ear. The <u>king</u> wore a crown. I <u>clung</u> on to the side of the boat.

Lesson #37- kn
Words: knack, knee, knew, knit, kneel, knot, knuckle, knife, knead, knob
Picture Box Sentence: I hit my knee on the knob.
Cloze Sentences: She <u>kneads </u>the bread. I <u>knit </u>a scarf for my mom. I scraped my <u>knuckle</u>.

Lesson #38 -mb
Words: comb, tomb, crumb, dumb
Picture Box Sentence: The comb is stuck in my hair.
Cloze Sentences: I ate the <u>crumbs</u> off the table. The mummy is in the <u>tomb</u>. There are no <u>dumb</u> questions.

Lesson #39 –tch*
Words: watch, catch, match, rematch, itch, hutch
Picture Box Sentence: I can catch the ball!
Cloze Sentences: The plant made me <u>itch</u>. The teams will have a <u>rematch</u>. Let's <u>watch</u> the movie.

Lesson #40 –dge (sounds like juh)
Words: badge, pledge, lodge, budge, bridge
Picture Box Sentence: We said the pledge in the lodge.
Cloze Sentences: I walked across the <u>bridge</u>. The door is stuck, and it won't <u>budge</u>. I earned a <u>badge</u>!

Lesson #41- soft g(sounds like juh)
Words: cage, rage, page, age, giant, danger, gentle
Picture Box Sentence: The giant dog was in a cage.
Cloze Sentences: The snake is in a <u>cage</u>. My <u>age</u> is ten years old. The bunny is <u>gentle</u>.

Lesson #42- soft c*
Words: ice, face, once, cent, since, circle, center, circus, saucer, special
Picture Box Sentence: The clown sat in the center of the circle.
Cloze Sentences: We saw a tiger at the <u>circus</u>. The <u>ice</u> melted. She had egg on her <u>face</u>.

Lesson #43- ail*
Words: bail, nail, snail, grail, mail, pail, rail, tail, trail, jail, sail
Picture Box Sentence: The snail in the pail had no tail.
Cloze Sentences: The thief is in <u>jail</u>. I hammered the <u>nail</u>. He delivers the <u>mail</u>.

Lesson #44- ain*
Words: brain, main, chain, gain, drain, grain, plain, strain, stain, train
Picture Box Sentence: The train carried grain across the plain.
Cloze Sentences: Water goes down a <u>drain</u>. My <u>brain</u> is tired from reading! I put a <u>chain</u> on my bike.

*Lesson #45- air**
Words: air, chair, fair, flair, hair, lair, pair, stairs
Picture Box Sentence: The monkey with purple hair sat in a chair.
Cloze Sentences: I have a <u>pair</u> of feet. The lion is in his <u>lair</u>. This is fresh <u>air</u>.

*Lesson # 46- all**
Words: all, ball, call, fall, hall, mall, stall, tall, wall
Picture Box Sentence: The ball went over the tall wall.
Cloze Sentences: There are a lot of stores at the <u>mall</u>. Don't <u>fall</u> off your bike! <u>All</u> the kids went to the park.

*Lesson #47- are (sounds like air)**
Words: bare, care, dare, fare, flare, mare, rare, scare, share, snare, spare, stare
Picture Box Sentence: A two-headed snake is very rare.
Cloze Sentences: It is nice to <u>share</u> your toys. The horse is a <u>mare</u>. She put the <u>spare</u> tire on the car.

*Lesson #48- ight**
Words: bright, fight, night, right, sight, tight, midnight, light, tonight
Picture Box Sentence: The firecrackers were bright in the night.
Cloze Sentences: The party is <u>tonight</u>, not tomorrow. I ate too much, and my pants are too <u>tight</u>! The children got into a <u>fight</u> over a game.

*Lesson #49- itch**
Words: itch, ditch, witch, switch, pitch, hitch, stitch
Picture Box Sentence: The witch must stitch her dress.
Cloze Sentences: The <u>witch</u> flew on a broom. The medicine made me <u>itch</u>. <u>Hitch</u> the horse to the wagon, please.

Lesson #50- ive (both short i and long i)
Words: give, live, alive, live, jive
Picture Box Sentence: I live in the city.
Cloze Sentences: The man is <u>alive </u>and well. Please <u>give</u> me a minute. I <u>live</u> on a boat.

*51- one (long o)**
Words: bone, cone, lone, shone, stone, tone, zone, alone
Picture Box Sentence: There was one cone on the tree.
Cloze Sentences: The sun <u>shone</u> in the sky. We were <u>alone</u> all day. The dog buried the <u>bone</u>.

*Lesson #52- ought**
Words: bought, brought, fought, sought, thought, ought
Picture Box Sentence: I thought I ought to buy it.
Cloze Sentences: I <u>bought</u> a book with my money. We <u>fought</u> over the book. I <u>thought </u>the book was funny.

Lesson #53- ure*
Words: cure, lure, pure, nature, mature, secure, endure, adventure, furniture
Picture Box Sentence: Our furniture was from nature.
Cloze Sentences: The ring was <u>pure</u> gold. Animals live in <u>nature</u>. Off the <u>furniture</u>!

Lesson #54- sc
Words: scab, scale, scan, scar, scare, school, scold, scout, scrap, scrape, scream, scum
Picture Box Sentence: The scum on the pond scared the scout.
Cloze Sentences: I <u>scream</u> when I am scared. The <u>scale</u> read seventy pounds. He has a <u>scab</u> on his knee.

Lesson #55- sk
Words: skate, skid, skill, skim, skin, skip, skinny, skirt, skit, skull, sky
Picture Box Sentence: The girl is tall and skinny.
Cloze Sentences: There are no clouds in the <u>sky</u>. You need <u>skills</u> to play basketball. I <u>skate</u> to school every day.

Lesson #56- sm
Words: smack, small, smart, smash, smear, smell, smile, smith, smock, smog, smoke, smooth, smug
Picture Box Sentence: I could smell smoke from the fire.
Cloze Sentences: What a pretty <u>smile</u> you have. <u>Smog</u> is dirty fog. <u>Smear</u> some jelly on the bread.

Lesson #57- sn
Words: snack, snail, snake, snap, snatch, snare, snarl, sneak, sniff, snob, snore, snort, snow, snub, snug
Picture Box Sentence: The snake ate a snack.
Cloze Sentences: I can't sleep because you <u>snore</u>! Let's <u>sneak</u> into the room. The dog <u>sniffs</u> the food.

Lesson #58- sp and spr
Words: space, spade, span, spank, spat, speak, spend, spike, spill, spit, split, spoke, spoon, spoil, spot, spray, spring, spurt
Picture Box Sentence: They had a little spat, but now they are friends again.
Cloze Sentences: <u>Spring</u> is my favorite season. I <u>speak</u> softly. An oil <u>spill</u> is a big problem.

Lesson #59- str
Words: strand, strange, stranger, strap, straw, stray, streak, stream, street, strict, string, struck, strong
Picture Box Sentence: The strange fish swam in the stream.
Cloze Sentences: There is a <u>streak</u> on the window. I am <u>strong</u> and healthy. The horses ate the <u>straw</u>.

Lesson #60- sw
Words: swam, swim, swum, swap, swarm, sway, sweat, sweet, swell, swift, swing, swish
Picture Box Sentence: The swine rolled in the mud.
Cloze Sentences: We <u>swim</u> in the river. The current may be <u>swift</u>. The candy is <u>sweet</u>.

Lesson #61- br
Words: brace, brad, brag, braid, brake, bran, brass, brat, brad, brew, brick, brim, broom, broke, brow
Picture Box Sentence: I broke the broom.
Cloze Sentences: She had three <u>braids</u> in her hair. The house was made of <u>brick</u>. <u>Bran</u> cereal is good for breakfast.

Lesson #62- cr
Words: crab, crack, craft, crate, crave, crawl, crazy, crew, crib, cried, cross, cry, crust, crop
Picture Box Sentence: The farmer grows a crop of corn.
Cloze Sentences: The pie has a <u>crust</u>. The baby will <u>crawl</u> across the room. The <u>crab</u> pinched my toe!

Lesson #63- dr
Words: drab, draft, drag, dragon, draw, dress, drift, drip, drool, drop, drum, dry
Picture Box Sentence: The dragon drooled on the drum.
Cloze Sentences: Her new <u>dress</u> is long. Can you <u>draw</u> a picture? The water <u>drips</u>.

Lesson #64- gr
Words: grab, grade, grain, gram, grate, gray, grill, grin, grime, grass, gross, grit, grunt
Picture Box Sentence: The gray grime on the grate is gross.
Cloze Sentences: I cut the <u>grass</u>. He picked it up with a <u>grunt</u>. We can cook on the <u>grill</u>.

Lesson #65- pr
Words: prank, pray, press, presto, pride, prim, prize, print, prod, prone, prong, promise, proud, prune, protect
Picture Box Sentence: First prize was a kiss on the cheek from your mom.
Cloze Sentences: Always keep your <u>promises</u>. I am <u>proud</u> of myself. The <u>prune</u> was wrinkled and black.

Lesson #66- tr
Words: trace, track, trade, train, trash, tray, tree, triangle, trick, trot, trouble, truck, true, try
Picture Box Sentence: The elephant swung his trunk into the tree.
Cloze Sentences: The <u>train</u> is coming! Always <u>try</u> your best. <u>Trash</u> belongs in the garbage.

Lesson #67- wr
Words: wrap, wrath, wreak, wreck, wren, wring, wrist, write, wrong, wrote
Picture Box Sentence: The beautiful wren sat in a tree and sang a song.
Cloze Sentences: I <u>wrote</u> my name on the paper. My watch is on my <u>wrist</u>. You are so <u>wrong</u>.

Lesson #68- bl
Words: blade, blank, blanket, blast, bleed, blend, bless, blew, blink, blind, bliss, blob, block, blubber, blot
Picture Box Sentence: The blanket covered the whale's blubber.
Cloze Sentences: The paper was <u>blank</u>. She <u>blew</u> her nose on her sleeve. The <u>blast</u> was loud.

Lesson #69- cl
Words: clad, claim, clam, clap, class, claw, clay, clean, click, climb, cling, closet, clothes, cloud, clumsy, clutter
Picture Box Sentence: The clumsy clam slipped on the clay.
Cloze Sentences: My <u>clothes</u> are dirty. We have twenty students in my <u>class</u>. I can <u>climb</u> on the rocks.

Lesson #70- fl
Words: flag, flake, flame, flap, flash, flat, fled, flesh, flick, float, flock, floor, flu, flush, fly
Picture Box Sentence: The flame burned the flesh of the fish.
Cloze Sentences: The dog sleeps on the <u>floor</u>. The <u>flag</u> is red, white and blue. She is sick with the <u>flu</u>.

Lesson #71- pl
Words: place, planet, plant, play, plod, plop, plug, plum, plush
Picture Box Sentence: The planet is in a far away place.
Cloze Sentences: She can <u>push</u> the stroller. I made a <u>plum</u> pie. The <u>plant</u> is green.

Lesson #72- sl
Words: slab, slack, slam, slant, slap, sled, sleepy, slice, slide, slims, slip, slop, slot, slow, slum, sly, slurp
Picture Box Sentence: The sleepy boy slows down.
Cloze Sentences: I <u>slice</u> the cake with a knife. We ride the <u>sled</u> in the snow. I should not <u>slurp</u> my soup.

Lesson #73 –sk(ending)*
Words: ask, bask, task, flask, mask, brisk, risk
Picture Box Sentence: The mask was purple and yellow.
Cloze Sentences: If you want something, <u>ask</u>. The cat likes to <u>bask</u> in the sun.

Lesson #74 –sp (ending)*
Words: clasp, grasp, rasp
Picture Box Sentence: I grasp the last piece of pizza from my sister.
Cloze Sentence: <u>Clasp</u> your hands together.

Lesson 75 –st (ending)*
Words: fast, past, best, fist, bust, dust, first, worst, least, exist
Picture Box Sentence: I hurt my fist on the jungle gym.
Cloze Sentences: There is <u>dust</u> on the table. I can run <u>fast</u>. He is my <u>best</u> friend.

Lesson #76 –nd (ending)*
Words: band, stand, bend, mend, bind, bond, pond
Picture Box Sentence: The dog jumped in the pond.
Cloze Sentences: I will <u>mend</u> the rip on my shirt. The <u>band</u> played at the football game. I don't like to <u>stand</u> still.

Lesson #77 –nk (ending)*
Words: bank, clank, ink, blink, bunk, chunk, junk, trunk
Picture Box Sentence: There is so much junk in his trunk!
Cloze Sentences: She had to <u>blink</u> her eyes. I spilled <u>ink</u> on the table. I put my money in the <u>bank</u>.

Lesson #78 –nt(ending)*
Words: ant, plant, bent, sent, went, hint, mint, tint, punt, runt
Picture Box Sentence: The tiny pig was the runt of the litter.
Cloze Sentences: I <u>went</u> to school. My mom drinks <u>mint</u> tea. The <u>ant</u> sat on the plant.

Lesson #79- ge (ending)*
Words: age, page, rage, stage, wage, barge, large, judge, fudge, bulge, range
Picture Box Sentence: The large judge ate fudge.
Cloze Sentences: The superstar walked onto the <u>stage</u>. Turn to the next <u>page</u> in your book. She earned a good <u>wage</u>.

Lesson #80 –mp(ending)*
Words: camp, damp, lamp, crimp, limp, bump, dump, plump, stump
Picture Box Sentence: We ate hot dogs on a stump at camp.
Cloze Sentences: I fell down and got a <u>bump</u> on my head. The <u>lamp</u> needs a light bulb. He <u>limps</u> because he hurt his leg.

See **Chapter 11 How to Teach Phonics Lessons**

STEP 2 PHONICS LESSONS (P2)

Lesson #81- short a
Words: rag, crash, trash, fact, branch, tax, cabin, grasp, blast, ax, brass, scrap, passenger
Picture Box Sentence: The branch fell onto the cabin.
Cloze Sentences: He used an <u>ax</u> to chop the wood. It is a <u>fact</u> that two plus two equals four. When you buy a car, you must pay <u>tax</u>.

Lesson #82- short e
Words: check, bet, held, sense, slept, crept, mend, rent, necklace, melt, sled, tent, gem, theft
Picture Box Sentence: The necklace started to melt in the sun.
Cloze Sentences: The tired baby <u>slept</u> soundly. Diamond is a precious <u>gem</u>. She <u>held</u> her arms up high.

Lesson #83- short i
Words: rid, limp, mist, sick, picnic, ticket, linen, zip, witch, pin, ditch, drill, mist, rich, digit
Picture Box Sentence: The sick witch held the ticket.
Cloze Sentences: The car drove into the <u>ditch</u>. The <u>rich</u> man had a lot of money. The <u>linen</u> jacket was wrinkled.

Lesson #84- short o
Words: knot, boss, toss, fond, rot, proper, hog, crop, October, pond, rob
Picture Box Sentence: The hog ate the crop of corn.
Cloze Sentences: Halloween is in <u>October</u>. There are fish in the <u>pond</u>. I have a <u>knot</u> in my shoelace.

Lesson #85- short u
Words: stuck, tunnel, funds, club, stuff, plum, subtract, hut, mud, bud,
Picture Box Sentence: The tunnel was full of mud.
Cloze Sentences: I can add and <u>subtract</u> in math. I am <u>stuck</u> in the house today. Do you like <u>plum</u> pudding?

Lesson #86- a/ final e*
Words: skate, frame, cave, stage, paste, trade, strange, daze, snake, escape, celebrate
Picture Box Sentence: The snake lives in a cold cave.
Cloze Sentences: Do you <u>celebrate</u> the holiday? The singers are on the <u>stage</u>. Don't eat <u>paste</u>!

Lesson #87- e/ final e
Words: eve, sphere, severe, these, here
Picture Box Sentence: The planet looks like a sphere.
Cloze Sentences: Here is the money. The severe weather was horrible. The ball is shaped like a sphere.

Lesson #88- i/ final e
Words: dine, pipe, hike, sometime, hire, pride, tribe, invite, provide, valentine, file.
Picture Box Sentence: The valentine card was pink and red.
Cloze Sentences: We had to hire a painter. Will you invite him to the party? The water in the pipe froze.

Lesson #89 - o/ final e
Words: stove, vote, cone, pole, rose, dove
Picture Box Sentence: She dove into the pool.
Cloze Sentences: I ate the ice cream cone. The stove is hot! The rose is beautiful.

Lesson #90- u/ final e
Words: huge, mule, cute, value, cube, produce, June
Picture Box Sentence: The huge mule ate a cube of sugar.
Cloze Sentences: His birthday is in June. The kitten is so cute! The house is a good value.

Lesson #91- ay
Words: bay, delay, halfway, display, payroll, relay
Picture Box Sentence: The goats ran a relay race.
Cloze Sentences: The display in the store window was amazing. Because of the delay, we missed the plane.

*Lesson #92- ai**
Words: aim, paint, maintain, faith, hail, straight, remain, rail, daisy, waiter, pail
Picture Box Sentence: The daisy was yellow and white.
Cloze Sentences: There is water in the pail. The hail fell from the sky. Did you paint the room blue?

*Lesson #93- ee**
Words: queen, reef, steel, sweep, beef, speech, agree, speech, speed, creek, seems, sleet, indeed, pioneer, knee, greedy, volunteer
Picture Box Sentence: The queen ate beef.
Cloze Sentences: The dog splashed in the creek. His speech was long and boring. The bridge was made out of steel.

Lesson #94- ie*
Words: niece, fierce, field, chief, frontier, briefcase
Picture Box Sentence: The chief put the cheese in her briefcase.
Cloze Sentences: The storm was <u>fierce.</u> My sister's daughter is my <u>niece</u>. The pioneers crossed the <u>frontier</u>.

Lesson #95- oa
Words: loan, groan, loaf, roast, oats, toast, roam
Picture Box Sentence: The tiger ate too much toast and roast.
Cloze Sentences: The horse ate the <u>oats</u>. I need a <u>loan</u> of ten dollars. All you do is moan and <u>groan</u>.

Lesson #96- ea*
Words: tea, pea, read, bead, least, beach, speak, tear, stream, read, neat, weave, please, reason, repeal, retreat, teaspoon, heap, beard
Picture Box Sentence: We drank tea on the beach.
Cloze Sentences: Would you pass the salt, <u>please</u>? Do you like to <u>read</u> books? He can <u>weave</u> blankets on his loom.

Lesson #97- ou
Words: outline, hour, county, wound, bound, proud, house, discount, outstanding, mountain
Picture Box Sentence: The house sat on the mountain.
Cloze Sentences: Dad is <u>proud</u> of me. We played for an <u>hour</u>. I <u>wound</u> the old clock.

Lesson #98- ow= long o
Words: sow, sparrow, vowel, towel, allow, coward, crown
Picture Box Sentence: The sparrow ate corn in the field.
Cloze Sentences: She won't <u>allow</u> that kind of behavior. The queen wore a <u>crown.</u> "E" is a <u>vowel</u>.

Lesson #99- oo
Words: shampoo, loose, soon, scooter, proof, toothbrush, tooth, foolish
Picture Box Sentence: He rode the scooter to school.
Cloze Sentences: They will be here <u>soon</u>. My tooth is <u>loose</u>. The <u>shampoo</u> smells nice.

Lesson 100- oy
Words: royal, employ, oyster, enjoy
Picture Box Sentence: The oyster sat on the beach.
Cloze Sentences: I <u>enjoy</u> reading. The <u>royal</u> family ate oysters.

Lesson #101- oi
Words: moist, choice, foil, spoil, appoint, disappoint, avoid
Picture Box Sentence: There is foil on the stove.
Cloze Sentences: They <u>spoil</u> their son. I try to <u>avoid</u> arguing. Her head felt <u>moist</u>.

Lesson #102- ew*
Words: chew, chewy, news, newspaper, knew, screw
Picture Box Sentence: The candy was chewy.
Cloze Sentences: Do you read the <u>newspaper</u>? Do you watch the <u>news</u>? <u>Chew</u> your food.

Lesson #103- ar
Words: cargo, artist, shark, charter, depart, darling, harm, carpet, marble, market, scarf, carton, harvest, grammar, art, tardy, particle, garden
Picture Box Sentence: The shark will harm the seals.
Cloze Sentences: The <u>artist</u> painted the picture. Tie a <u>scarf</u> around your neck. The <u>carpet</u> was stained and dirty.

Lesson #104- or
Words: former, oral, tornado, visitor, support, border, fort, pork, favor, honor, mayor, refrigerator, ignore, force, horse, order, organize, forest, junior
Picture Box Sentence: The tornado blew the refrigerator into the forest.
Cloze Sentences: The <u>mayor</u> gave a speech. I like to ride my <u>horse</u> in the morning. You can't <u>force</u> someone to be your friend.

Lesson #105- ir
Words: firm, thirsty, first, third, skirt, dirty, Virginia
Picture Box Sentence: I bought the skirt in Virginia.
Cloze Sentences: If you are <u>thirsty</u>, drink some water. He was <u>third</u> and earned a bronze medal. This room is <u>dirty</u>.

Lesson #106- ur
Words: jury, hamburger, blur, turnip, nurse, surf, turkey, surface, burst, hurricane, curl
Picture Box Sentence: The hamburger was made from turkey.
Cloze Sentences: The <u>hurricane</u> destroyed the island, The <u>nurse</u> will help the patient. The judge spoke to the <u>jury</u>.

Lesson #107- er
Words: perfect, terrific, herd, dryer, cover, government, adverb, tender, under, eraser, rubber, mercy, wonder, perfume, merchant, clover, blender, water
Picture Box Sentence: The eraser was made of rubber.
Cloze Sentences: Slowly is an <u>adverb</u>. I <u>wonder</u> what is in the box? A dryer is the <u>perfect</u> gift!

Lesson #108- ch
Words: chair, cherry, chestnut, cheetah, chief, chamber, champion, challenge, chalk, China, chocolate, chubby, chimney, chimpanzee, children
Picture Box Sentence: The children loved the chubby chimpanzee.
Cloze Sentences: The <u>cheetah</u> is the fastest animal on earth. The <u>cherry</u> pie is yummy. Sometimes it is a <u>challenge</u> to do your best.

Lesson #109- sh
Words: shrimp, shorten, shuffle, shoulder, shrink, shrine, shudder, shun, shutter
Picture Box Sentence: The shortstop hurt her shoulder.
Cloze Sentences: Close the <u>shutter</u>! If you <u>shorten</u> the rope, you can use it as a belt. The <u>shrimp</u> are tiny and pink.

Lesson #110- th
Words: theft, thermometer, theory, thicken, thigh, thousand, thrash, throb, thimble, thrown
Picture Box Sentence: We threw a thousand thimbles into the water.
Cloze Sentences: I hurt my <u>thigh</u> on the jungle gym. I read your temperature on the <u>thermometer</u>.

Lesson #111- wh
Words: whirlpool, whichever, whomever, whale, whey, whole, white, whirlwind
Picture Box Sentence: The white-tailed dove is a lovely bird.
Cloze Sentences: I ate the <u>whole</u> thing! Little Miss Muffet ate curds and <u>whey</u>. The clam went down the <u>whirlpool</u>.

Lesson #112 –ck(ending)
Words: deadlock, sidekick, struck, amuck, carsick, rickrack, henpeck, gimmick, maverick
Picture Box Sentence: The whole family looked carsick.
Cloze Sentences: We <u>struck</u> a pose. The <u>gimmick</u> worked: they bought the car. The superhero had a <u>sidekick.</u>

Lesson #113 -ng
Words: mustang, overhang, headlong, slang, string, oblong, prolong, awning, boomerang
Picture Box Sentence: The awning kept the sun off the house.
Cloze Sentences: Mom does not know <u>slang</u>. The <u>boomerang</u> came back to me. The wild <u>mustang</u> ran free.

Lesson #114- gn
Words: gnu, gnarl, gnaw, gnat, gnome
Picture Box Sentence: The gnome sat in the garden.
Cloze Sentences: There is a <u>gnat</u> on the fruit. The <u>gnu</u> is a kind of antelope. My dog <u>gnaws</u> on the bone.

Lesson #115- kn
Words: knot, knowledge, knee, kneecap, knighthood, knoll, knives, knapsack
Picture Box Sentence: The knight hurt his kneecap.
Cloze Sentences: The knives are sharp. There are tools in the knapsack. Do you have knowledge of the crime?

Lesson #116- pn
Word: pneumonia
Picture Box Sentence: I was sick with pneumonia.
Cloze Sentence: I took medicine when I had pneumonia.

Lesson #117- mn
Words: hymn, condemn, column, plumb, climb
Picture Box Sentence: We sang the hymn together.
Cloze Sentences: Can you climb the tree? The column is tall and straight. The line is plumb.

Lesson #118- tch
Words: butcher, outmatch, unlatch, hitch, dispatch, patch, backstitch
Picture Box Sentence: The butcher put the meat in the freezer.
Cloze Sentences: The big kids outmatch the little kids. I will unlatch the door. I sewed on my patch.

Lesson #119- dge
Words: budget, hodgepodge, knowledge
Picture Box Sentence: Tonight, dinner is a hodgepodge.
Cloze Sentences: Do you have knowledge of the event? Our budget for the party is $20.

Lesson #120- soft g
Words: gentleman, Germany, manager, imagine, package, emergency, dangerous, general
Picture Box Sentence: A package arrived from Germany.
Cloze Sentences: The manager works hard. The gentleman was never rude. It is good to be calm in an emergency.

Lesson #121- soft c
Words: notice, dancer, cereal, ceiling, exercise, success, cylinder, recent, Pacific, central, accident, lace, officer, balance, cement, ceremony, ceramic
Picture Box Sentence: I threw cereal on the ceiling for exercise.
Cloze Sentences: Can you balance on the plank? The dancer jumps and twirls. The scarf is made of lace.

Lesson #122- ail
Words: ponytail, hangnail, toenail, fingernail, prevail, airmail, detail, monorail
Picture Box Sentence: We rode the monorail up the mountain.
Cloze Sentences: The <u>detail</u> on the painting is amazing! He had gross green <u>toenails</u> and <u>fingernails</u>.

Lesson #123- ain
Words: terrain, complain, entertain, explain, maintain, refrain, domain, eyestrain, attain
Picture Box Sentence: The terrain was rough and dangerous.
Cloze Sentences: I got <u>eyestrain</u> from looking at the computer all day. The performers love to <u>entertain</u>.

Lesson #124- air
Words: stair, armchair, despair, wheelchair, flair, fair
Picture Box Sentence: There were fireworks at the fair.
Cloze Sentences: She played basketball in the <u>wheelchair</u>. Have a seat in that <u>armchair</u>. Don't <u>despair</u>, everything will be fine.

Lesson #125- all
Words: snowball, football, squall, befall, install, overall, meatball, snowfall
Picture Box Sentence: We played football with a huge snowball.
Cloze Sentences: The workers will <u>install</u> a new floor today. The <u>squall</u> ruined the boating trip. <u>Overall</u>, we had a good time.

Lesson #126- are(sounds like air)
Words: aware, airfare, compare, beware, prepare, nightmare, hardware, ensnare, fanfare
Picture Box Sentence: There was much fanfare at the parade.
Cloze Sentences: <u>Compare</u> prices before you purchase a ticket. The <u>airfare</u> cost $650! I had a <u>nightmare</u> and couldn't fall back asleep.

Lesson #127- ay
Words: freeway, dismay, payday, betray, anyway, relay, subway, foray, gateway, holiday
Picture Box Sentence: The subway was full of tired people.
Cloze Sentences: Thanksgiving is my favorite <u>holiday</u>. The cars drove on the <u>freeway</u>. She will get money on <u>payday</u>.

Lesson #128- ight
Words: twilight, daylight, copyright, alright, highlight, hindsight, airtight, plight, delight
Picture Box Sentence: The copyright is at the bottom of this page.
Cloze Sentences: The baby will <u>delight</u> his grandmother. The <u>highlight</u> of the trip was the boat ride. We ate dinner in the <u>twilight</u>.

Lesson #129- itch

Words: hitch, unhitch, bewitch, stitch, backstitch, switch
Picture Box Sentence: The witch unhitched her dragon from the wagon.
Cloze Sentences: I will <u>switch</u> the signs, and nobody will know. The tailor will <u>stitch</u> the dress.

Lesson #130- ive (long and short)

Words: active, survive, attractive, positive, relative, connive, creative, revive
Picture Box Sentence: The attractive model posed for the camera.
Cloze Sentences: Dad tried to <u>revive</u> the sick plant. A <u>positive</u> attitude will take you far. We want to be healthy and <u>active</u>.

Lesson #131- one

Words: telephone, wishbone, prone, headphone, postpone, limestone, acetone, flagstone
Picture Box Sentence: The fireplace was made of white limestone.
Cloze Sentences: Is that the <u>telephone</u> ringing? <u>Acetone</u> is a chemical. She was sick and had to <u>postpone</u> the appointment.

Lesson #132- ought

Words: ought, sought, drought (ow)
Picture Box Sentence: I thought I ought to try it.
Cloze Sentence: The <u>drought</u> was over once it rained.

Lesson #133- ure

Words: furniture, adventure, temperature, secure, endure, mature
Picture Box Sentence: The furniture was old and dirty.
Cloze Sentences: He is <u>mature</u> for his age. What an exciting <u>adventure</u>! The <u>temperature</u> is 107 degrees.

Lesson #134- tion

Words: education, conversation, lotion, nation, direction, vacation, fiction, information, pollution, instruction, multiplication
Picture Box Sentence: I squirted the lotion in your direction.
Cloze Sentences: They had a long phone <u>conversation</u>. We went to the beach on our <u>vacation</u>. Do you like <u>fiction</u> or nonfiction?

Lesson #135- sion

Words: television, explosion, compassion, decision, discussion, depression, mission, confusion, tension, vision
Picture Box Sentence: The explosion caused a lot of damage.
Cloze Sentences: Sometimes it is hard to make the right <u>decision</u>. He never turns on the <u>television</u>. Martin Luther King, Jr. had a <u>vision</u> of the future.

Lesson #136- ious
Words: delicious, curious, serious
Picture Box Sentence: The turnip and beet cupcake was delicious.
Cloze Sentences: Are you <u>serious</u>? The <u>curious</u> cat fell into the pond. I ate the <u>delicious</u> food.

Lesson #137- ous
Words: tremendous, generous, nervous, humorous
Picture Box Sentence: A tremendous tree fell on the car.
Cloze Sentences: The television show was very <u>humorous</u>. He was scared and <u>nervous</u> all day. A car is a <u>generous</u> gift.

Lesson #138- ence
Words: fence, difference, sequence
Picture Box Sentence: The fence was twenty feet high.
Cloze Sentences: The dance follows a <u>sequence</u> of steps. There is a big <u>difference</u> between trying and trying your best.

Lesson #139- ance*
Words: ambulance, entrance, trance, ignorance, dance, fragrance, stance
Picture Box Sentence: The flower had a lovely fragrance.
Cloze Sentences: The dance follows a <u>sequence</u> of steps. The <u>ambulance</u> is speeding down the road. This is the exit, please go to the <u>entrance</u>.

Lesson #140- ph
Words: graph, photo, photograph, phase, phone, telephone, triumph, phase, phrase
Picture Box Sentence: I have a photograph of my parents' wedding.
Cloze Sentences: Please <u>phone</u> your mom at home. Eating glue is a <u>phase</u> for the kindergartner. The <u>graph</u> shows that sales are up this year.

Lesson #141- ion= yun
Words: billion, million, trillion, union, rebellion, onion, scallion, companion
Picture Box Sentence: There are a billion stars in the sky.
Cloze Sentences: The pirates staged a <u>rebellion</u>. My dog is my faithful <u>companion</u>. The <u>onion</u> made me cry.

Lesson #142- qu= kwa
Words: question, quote, quiz, quick, quit, quite, quest, quart, quail, queasy, quench, quack
Picture Box Sentence: The slimy juice made me quite queasy.
Cloze Sentences: The teacher gave us a <u>quiz</u>. I asked my sister a <u>question</u>. <u>Quick</u>! What is two times seven?

See *Chapter 11 How to Teach Phonics Lessons*

STEP 3 PHONICS LESSONS (P3)

Your child is expected to read these words by the end of the 5th grade. Many of the words found in these phonics lessons combine two or more phonics concepts. For example, *microwave* contains *long i, long o, long a* and *cr (* blend), any of which might cause difficulty. If your child is unable to read a group of Step 3 words, try to determine which phonics concepts are problematic, and then review the corresponding Step 1 and Step 2 phonics lessons before returning to Step 3 lessons.

Lesson #143- long a
Words: indicate, sane, educate, calculate, gale, microwave, create, migrate, demonstrate
Picture Sentence: The food in the microwave was moldy.
Cloze Sentences: I will create a masterpiece. The animals will migrate this winter. Can you calculate the cost?

Lesson #144- long e
Words: severe, hemisphere, supreme
Picture Sentence: She thinks she is the supreme queen.
Cloze Sentences: We live in the Northern hemisphere. I have a severe headache.

Lesson #145- long i
Words: appetite, polite, device, excite, describe, emphasize, unite, turnpike, inquire
Picture Sentence: His appetite is so huge that he can eat an elephant.
Cloze Sentences: The truck is on the turnpike. Saying please is very polite. Use the device to open the can.

Lesson #146- long o
Words: oppose, quote, zone, globe, stroke, telescope, expose
Picture Sentence: We will expose the film in the sun.
Cloze Sentences: She looked in the telescope and saw the moon. I found the mountain range on the globe. I oppose that law because it is unjust.

Lesson #147- long u
Words: assume, intrude, issue, volume, rescue, pure
Picture Sentence: Turn up the volume!
Cloze Sentences: They will rescue the dog from the pond. The ring is pure gold. Don't assume anything.

Lesson #148- ay
Words: payment, layman, decay, portray, delay, layer, essay, frayed
Picture Sentence: The cake had five layers.
Cloze Sentences: The hem of the pants is <u>frayed</u>. She made a <u>payment</u> on the house. I wrote an <u>essay</u> on democracy.

Lesson #149- ai
Words: entertain, acquaint, prairie, plain, gait, failure, aide, aid, frail, despair
Picture Sentence: The singer will entertain the troops.
Cloze Sentences: <u>Acquaint</u> yourself with the rules. I like <u>plain</u> noodles, without sauce. The frail horse had a bad <u>gait</u>.

Lesson #150- ee
Words: freedom, need, keel, leer, committee, leech
Picture Sentence: The rules were made by a committee of one.
Cloze Sentences: Do you <u>need</u> anything else? The color will <u>leech</u> out of the cloth. The soldiers fight for <u>freedom</u>.

Lesson #151- ie
Words: species, relieve, frontier, lien, shield, shriek, belief
Picture Sentence: No one had ever seen that <u>species</u> of dog.
Cloze Sentences: We crossed the frontier in wagons. She wore a shield in battle. There was a <u>lien</u> against the house.

Lesson #152- oa
Words: approach, cocoa, goal, coal, boast
Picture Sentence: I put cocoa in the milk.
Cloze Sentences: He likes to brag and <u>boast</u>. The <u>goal</u> is to win the game. <u>Approach</u> the rabid dog carefully.

Lesson #153- ea(short and long e)
Words: reveal, impeach, defeat, cease, European, deaf, jealous, meadow
Picture Sentence: They wanted to impeach the European president.
Cloze Sentences: They will never <u>defeat</u> our superior team. Don't be <u>jealous</u> of my good luck. A good reporter never <u>reveals</u> her sources.

Lesson #154- ou
Words: outnumbered, pout, council, encounter, pouch, announce, boundary, outburst
Picture Sentence: The fat baby began to <u>pout</u>.
Cloze Sentences: There is gold in the <u>pouch</u>. I will <u>announce</u> the good news. That team is <u>outnumbered</u>.

Lesson #155- ow (long o)
Words: owner, ownership, burrow
Picture Sentence: The owner of the broken vase began to scream loudly.
Cloze Sentences: The prairie dog began to dig a burrow. Home ownership is not easy.

Lesson #156- ow
Words: towering, drowsy, Mayflower
Picture Sentence: The drowsy pig fell asleep.
Cloze Sentences: The trees are towering over the house. The drowsy pig fell asleep. Their family came to America on the Mayflower.

Lesson #157- oo(oo and short u)
Words: groove, statehood, mood, textbook, misunderstood, nook, booming, bamboo, woodland, loom outlook
Picture Sentence: The textbook weighed twenty pounds!
Cloze Sentences: I have a cozy reading nook. The furniture is made from bamboo. She is always so misunderstood.

Lesson #158- oy
Words: royalty, destroy, boycott, loyal, convoy
Picture Sentence: The convoy traveled across the plains.
Cloze Sentences: You are a true and loyal friend. We will boycott that diner because they mistreat their employees.

Lesson #159- oi
Words: viewpoint, Illinois, recoil, rejoice, avoid, appoint, hoist, avoidance
Picture Sentence: When we heard the good news, we rejoiced.
Cloze Sentences: Avoid dangerous situations. She was born in Illinois. My viewpoint makes much more sense.

Lesson #160- ew
Words: news, view, chewy
Picture Sentence: The meat was tough and chewy.
Cloze Sentences: The penthouse view is spectacular. Did you hear the news?

Lesson #161- ar
Words: altar, arch, charter, ark, startle, remark, architect, molar, familiar, peculiar, snarl
Picture Sentence: The rabid dog began to snarl.
Cloze Sentences: The architect designed the house. The church has an altar. That is a peculiar way of doing things.

Lesson #162- or
Words: ancestor, editor, advisor, superior, conductor, nor, historian, director, performance, ordinary, navigator, ornamental
Picture Sentence: This is no ordinary performance.
Cloze Sentences: The <u>historian</u> knew all about the president. The newspaper <u>editor</u> makes the final decisions. The <u>director</u> yelled, "Cut!"

Lesson #163- ir
Words: circumstance, thirsty, Virginia
Picture Sentence: The thirsty gorilla drank the soda.
Cloze Sentences: The president lives in <u>Virginia</u>. We are unsure of his <u>circumstances</u>.

Lesson #164- ur
Words: urban, current, plural, pluralism, surplus, rural, urge
Picture Sentence: She had an urge to laugh out loud.
Cloze Sentences: I live in Chicago, an <u>urban</u> environment. My cousin lives on a farm in a <u>rural</u> environment. The <u>current</u> government is popular.

Lesson #165- er
Words: avert, barrier, perk, performance, terms, derby, concern, merchant
Picture Sentence: They erected a barrier at the entrance.
Cloze Sentences: What are the <u>terms</u> of the agreement? I have a <u>concern</u> about your school work. I will <u>avert</u> my eyes when the monster is revealed.

Lesson #166- soft ch
Words: champagne, chancellor, chinchilla, chaplain, chauffeur, chivalry
Picture Sentence: The chinchilla was soft and cuddly.
Cloze Sentences: The <u>chauffeur</u> gets paid to drive. The <u>chaplain</u> lead the prayer. The <u>chancellor</u> of the university is highly respected.

167- hard ch
Words: chemist, chemistry, cholesterol, chlorine, chemical, chromosome, chronological
Picture Sentence: The children stood in chronological order.
Cloze Sentences: She wanted a <u>chemistry</u> set. The pool is full of <u>chlorine</u>. His <u>cholesterol</u> is low because he exercises and eats healthfully.

Lesson #168- sh
Words: shortening, sheriff, shellac, sherbet,
Picture Sentence: The hungry sheriff ate lime sherbet.
Cloze Sentences: We will finish the table with a layer of <u>shellac</u>. I added <u>shortening</u> to the recipe.

Lesson #169- th
Words: thesaurus, theme, thesis
Picture Sentence: The thesaurus contained five thousand words.
Cloze Sentences: I wrote my <u>thesis</u> paper on difficult subject. The <u>theme</u> of the play is love.

Lesson #170- wh
Words: whirlpool, whichever, whomever, whale, whey, whole, white, whirlwind
Picture Box Sentence: The white-tailed dove is a lovely bird.
Cloze Sentences: I ate the <u>whole</u> thing! Little Miss Muffet ate curds and <u>whey</u>. The clam went down the <u>whirlpool</u>.

Lesson #171- gn
Words: gnu, gnarl, gnaw, gnat, gnome
Picture Box Sentence: The gnu laughed.
Cloze Sentences: There is a <u>gnat</u> on the fruit. The <u>gnu</u> is a kind of antelope. My dog <u>gnaws</u> on the bone.

Lesson #172- kn
Words: knot, knowledge, knee, kneecap, knighthood, knoll, knives, knapsack
Picture Box Sentence: The knot was as big as my head.
Cloze Sentences: The <u>knives</u> are sharp. There are tools in the <u>knapsack</u>. Do you have <u>knowledge</u> of the crime?

Lesson #173- pn
Word: pneumonia, pneumatic
Picture Box Sentence: Pneumonia can be deadly.
Cloze Sentence: I took medicine when I had <u>pneumonia</u>.

Lesson #174- mn
Words: hymn, condemn, column, mnemonic
Picture Box Sentence: We sang the hymn and read the column.
Cloze Sentences: I read the <u>newspaper</u> column. We sang the <u>hymn</u> in church. The thief is <u>condemned</u> to jail.

Lesson #175- tch
Words: butcher, outmatch, unlatch, hitch, dispatch, patch, backstitch
Picture Box Sentence: The patch covered her eye.
Cloze Sentences: The big kids <u>outmatch</u> the little kids. I will <u>unlatch</u> the door. I sewed on my <u>patch</u>.

Lesson #176- dge
Words: budget, hodgepodge, knowledge
Picture Box Sentence: Tonight, dinner is a hodgepodge.
Cloze Sentences: Do you have <u>knowledge</u> of the event? Our <u>budget</u> for the party is $20.

Lesson #177- soft g
Words: generation, emerge, bulge, margin, voyage, encourage, rigid, legend, fringe, energetic, exaggerate
Picture Box Sentence: The ship set sail on the voyage.
Cloze Sentences: The butterfly began to <u>emerge</u> from the cocoon. I try to <u>encourage</u> my friends to do their best. He always <u>exaggerates</u> his injuries.

Lesson #178- soft c
Words: innocent, cycle, intelligence, cancel, precise, civil, evidence
Picture Box Sentence: The police officer searched for evidence.
Cloze Sentences: The actress decided to <u>cancel</u> the play. I didn't do it, I swear I am <u>innocent!</u> You must be neat and <u>precise</u> in your work.

Lesson #179- ail
Words: ail, travail, ponytail, hangnail, toenail, fingernail, prevail, airmail, detail, monorail
Picture Box Sentence: The letter arrived by airmail.
Cloze Sentences: The <u>detail</u> on the painting is amazing! Work hard and you will <u>prevail</u>.

Lesson #180- ain
Words: ascertain, terrain, entertain, explain, maintain, refrain, domain, eyestrain, attain
Picture Box Sentence: I ascertain that the situation is dangerous.
Cloze Sentences: I got <u>eyestrain</u> from looking at the computer all day. The performers love to <u>entertain</u>. Please <u>explain</u> the directions.

Lesson #181- air
Words: stair, armchair, despair, wheelchair, flair, fair
Picture Box Sentence: She has a flair with words.
Cloze Sentences: She played basketball in the <u>wheelchair</u>. Have a seat in that <u>armchair</u>. Don't <u>despair</u>, everything will be fine.

Lesson #182- all
Words: appall, forestall, snowball, football, squall, befall, install, overall, meatball, snowfall
Picture Box Sentence: The meatball was brown and juicy.
Cloze Sentences: We were <u>appalled</u> by the crime. The <u>squall</u> ruined the boating trip. Who knows what will <u>befall</u> the man now?

Lesson #183- are(sounds like air)
Words: threadbare, welfare, compare, beware, prepare, nightmare, hardware, ensnare, fanfare
Picture Box Sentence: His clothes were patched and threadbare.
Cloze Sentences: Compare prices before you purchase a ticket. The airfare cost $650! Your safety and welfare are important to me.

Lesson #184- ight
Words: twilight, daylight, copyright, alright, highlight, hindsight, airtight, plight, delight
Picture Box Sentence: Alright, alright, you can have a bite!
Cloze Sentences: Today we learned about the plight of African elephants. The highlight of the trip was the boat ride. We ate dinner in the twilight.

Lesson #185- itch
Words: hitch, unhitch, bewitch, stitch, backstitch, switch
Picture Box Sentence: Unhitch the wagon and let the horse run free.
Cloze Sentences: We will switch places. Can you stitch a new coat?

Lesson #186- ive
Words: native, motive, incentive, persuasive, protective, alternative, competitive
Picture Box Sentence: The salesman was very persuasive.
Cloze Sentences: The mother bear is protective towards her cubs. The suspect had no motive. I need a better incentive to work that hard.

Lesson #187- one
Words: silicone, ozone, monotone, cortisone, postpone, backbone
Picture Box Sentence: The silicone oozed onto the floor.
Cloze Sentences: The boring speaker talks in a monotone voice. The groom decided to postpone the wedding. The doctor gave her a cortisone injection to reduce the swelling.

Lesson #188- ought
Words: wrought, bethought, thought
Picture Box Sentence: The fence was made from wrought iron.
Cloze Sentences: I thought I saw a pussy cat.

Lesson #189- ure
Words: insecure, demure, pedicure, impure, allure, coiffure, obscure
Picture Box Sentence: His coiffure took ten hours to create.

Cloze Sentences: Jumping out of an airplane holds a certain <u>allure</u>. The <u>insecure</u> baby holds onto her mother all day. He always lives in such <u>obscure</u> places.

Lesson #190- tion
Words: plantation, tradition, infection, destination, exploration, communication, humiliation, section, expectation, constitution, humiliation
Picture Box Sentence: The sugar cane plantation was turned into a resort hotel.
Cloze Sentences: Good <u>communication</u> will prevent misunderstandings. The <u>constitution</u> was written by the country's founders. My parents have high <u>expectations</u>.

Lesson #191- sion(sounds like shun)
Words: invasion, corrosion, emission, confession, version, admission, tension, dimension, expansion, comprehension, collision, collusion, inspection
Picture Box Sentence: The invasion of the ants into the termite colony was alarming.
Cloze Sentences: The two speeding cars had a <u>collision</u>. The <u>inspection</u> revealed that the car had harmful <u>emissions</u>.

Lesson #192- ious
Words: mysterious, furious, infectious, precious, ferocious, luscious, ambitious, nutritious, glorious, various, superstitious, repetitious
Picture Box Sentence: The soft and cuddly bunny was actually a ferocious and dangerous animal.
Cloze Sentences: Vegetables are <u>nutritious</u>. My mom is <u>furious</u> because I came home late. The <u>ambitious</u> worker volunteered for extra work.

Lesson #193- ous
Words: numerous, miraculous, prosperous, enormous,
Picture Box Sentence:
Cloze Sentences: The couple worked very hard, and now they are <u>prosperous</u>. That boy has an <u>enormous</u> head. Her stories are too <u>numerous</u> to count.

Lesson #194- ence
Words: residence, consequence, coincidence, reference
Picture Box Sentence: The residence was a mansion on a private island.
Cloze Sentences: Please consider the <u>consequence</u> of your decision. Isn't it a <u>coincidence</u> that we have the same name?

Lesson #195- ance
Words: endurance, France, advance, romance, grievance, prance, arrogance, ordinance, finance, tolerance
Picture Box Sentence: The letter was full of love and romance.
Cloze Sentences: I have no <u>tolerance</u> for lying. We went to <u>France</u> last summer. The horse began to <u>prance</u> around the ring.

See *Chapter 11 How to Teach Phonics Lessons*

WORDS FOR WORD WHEELS

Lesson #1- short a
at: hat, fat, cat, sat, mat, bat, rat
an: man, fan, ran

Lesson #2- short e
et: let, bet, wet, get, set, jet, met
ell: tell, well, fell, smell

Lesson #3- short i
it: bit, fit, sit, lit
ill: will, fill, sill, till

Lesson #7- long o
o: so, go, no
old: cold, mold, fold, hold, told, sold

Lesson #8- long a/ final e
ame: came, name, blame
ake: take, make, rake, sake, bake, snake, fake
ade: made, shade, grade
ate: late, gate, date, rate, fate
ase; chase, case, base
ace: brace, face, lace

Lesson #10- long i/ final e
ive; five, live, jive, dive, drive
ine: nine, fine, mine, shine, line
ide: wide, ride, hide, slide
ime: time, dime, lime, slime
ite: bite, kite, mite
ile: smile, pile, mile, awhile

Lesson #11- long o
ose: close, hose, rose, nose, those
one: bone, stone, alone, phone

Lesson #13- ay
ay: day, play, way, say, slay, lay, may, gray, stay, away, pay, hay, fray

Lesson #14- ai
ain: rain, chain, train, brain, plain, stain
air: fair, hair, stair, pair, chair

Lesson #15- ee
ee: see, tree, bee, three
eed: seed, need, feed
eek: week, cheek, creek, seek

Lesson #17- oa
oad: road, toad, load
oat: goat, boat, moat, coat, float, throat

Lesson #18- ea
ear: dear, fear, near, year, clear
ean: clean, mean, lean, bean
eat: seat, feat, treat, cheat, meat

Lesson #19- ou
our: sour, hour, flour
ound: round, ground, found, mound

Lesson #20- ow
ow: now, cow, bow, how, chow

Lesson #21- ow= long o
ow: low, bow, know, blow, show, grow, window

Lesson #22- oo
oon: soon, moon, noon, spoon, balloon

Lesson #23- oy
oy: boy, toy, joy, enjoy

Lesson #25- ew
ew: dew, new, few, blew, knew, drew, grew, flew, threw

Lesson #26- ar
art: cart, fart, tart, start, smart, chart

Lesson #35- ck
ack: sack, back, black, pack, tack, track
eck: check, deck, fleck, heck, neck, peck, speck, wreck
ick: brick, chick, sick, crick, flick, kick, lick, nick, pick, prick, quick, slick, stick, thick, tick, trick, wick
ock: block, crock, clock, dock, frock, flock, knock, lock, rock, shock, smock, sock, stock

uck: buck, chuck, cluck, duck, luck, pluck, snuck, stuck, suck, tuck

Lesson #36- ng (ending)
ang- fang, bang, gang, hand, rang
ing: ring, ding, king, sing, sting, thing, wing
ong: bong, gong, long, song, prong, strong, thong, tong, wrong, along
ung: clung, sung, flung, lung, rung, slung, wrung

Lesson #39- tch
atch: catch, latch, match, patch, snatch, thatch
itch: ditch, glitch, hitch, pitch, snitch, stitch, switch, witch

Lesson #42- soft c
ice: mice, nice, rice, twice

Lesson #43- ail
ail: fail, grail, mail, sail, hail, jail, nail, pail, rail, snail, tail, trail

Lesson #44- ain
ain: brain, main, chain, gain, drain grain, plain, stain, train

Lesson #45- air
air- chair, fair, flair, hair, lair, pair, stair

Lesson #46- all
all: ball, call, fall, hall, mall, stall, tall, wall

Lesson #47- are (sounds like air)
are: bare, blare, dare, fare, flare, hare, mare, pare, rare, scare, share, snare, spare, stare

Lesson #48- ight
ight: bright, blight, fight, night, right, sight, tight

Lesson #49- itch
itch: ditch, hitch, pitch, stitch, switch, witch

Lesson #51- one
one: bone, cone, crone, lone, shone, stone, tone, zone, alone

Lesson #52- ought
ought: bought, brought, fought, sought, thought

Lesson #53- ure
ure: cure, lure, pure

Lesson #73- sk
ask: bask, task, flask, mask

Lesson #74- sp
asp: clasp, grasp, rasp

Lesson #75- st
est: best, chest, crest, guest, jest, nest, pest, quest, rest, vest, west, wrest, zest
ist: fist, gist, list, mist, wrist
ust: crust, dust, bust, dust, gust, just, must, rust, thrust, trust
oast: coast, boast, roast, toast

Lesson #76- nd
and: band, bland, brand, gland, grand, hand, land, sand, stand, strand
end: blend, fend, lend, mend, send, spend, tend, trend
ind: blind, find, grind, hind, kind, mind, rind, wind

Lesson #77- nk
ank: bank, blank, clank, crank, dank, drank, flank, frank, lank, plank, prank, rank, sank, shrank, stank, spank, swank, tank, thank, yank
ink: blink, brink, chink, clink, drink, fink, kink, link, mink, pink, rink, sink, shrink, slink, think, wink
unk: bunk, chunk, clunk, drunk, dunk, flunk, funk, hunk, junk, plunk, shrunk, skunk, slunk, spunk, stunk, trunk
ant: can't, chant, grant, pant, plant, rant, scant, slant

Lesson #78- nt
ent: bent, cent, sent, spent, tent, went
int: dint, flint, glint, hint, lint, mint, print, splint, sprint, squint, stint, tint
unt: punt, runt, shunt

Lesson #79- ge (sounds like juh)
age: cage, page, rage, stage, wage
udge; judge, fudge, pudge

Lesson #80- mp
amp: camp, cramp, clamp, damp, lamp, ramp, scamp, stamp, tramp
ump: bump, chump; clump, dump, frump, grump, hump, jump, lump, pump, plump, slump, stump, stump, thump, trump

Lesson # 86- long a/ final e
ame: fame, frame, same, lame, name, tame
ave: cave, brave, grave, behave, save

Lesson #92- ai
ain: gain, pain, main, grain, contain, plain, brain
ail: pail, jail, mail, trail, tail

Lesson #93- ee
eek: creek, seek, peek
eed: weed, bleed, speed

Lesson #94- ie
ief: chief, thief, brief, relief

Lesson #96- ea
each: beach, peach, reach, preach
eal: real, seal, deal, steal

Lesson #102- ew
ew: knew, screw, chew

Lesson #139- ance
ance: glance, dance, trance, stance, France

Phonics Introduction Lesson Page

Lesson #_____

Introduction to:

Words:

_____   _____

_____   _____

_____   _____

_____   _____

_____   _____

Cloze Sentences:

_____

_____

_____

Word Wheel

Directions:
1. Cut out circles on dotted lines.
2. Place smaller circle over larger circle.
3. Poke hole through center mark with brass brad.
4. Write rime on inside circle.
5. Write onsets on outside lines.
Be careful to write toward center.
Top circle should turn smoothly.

example

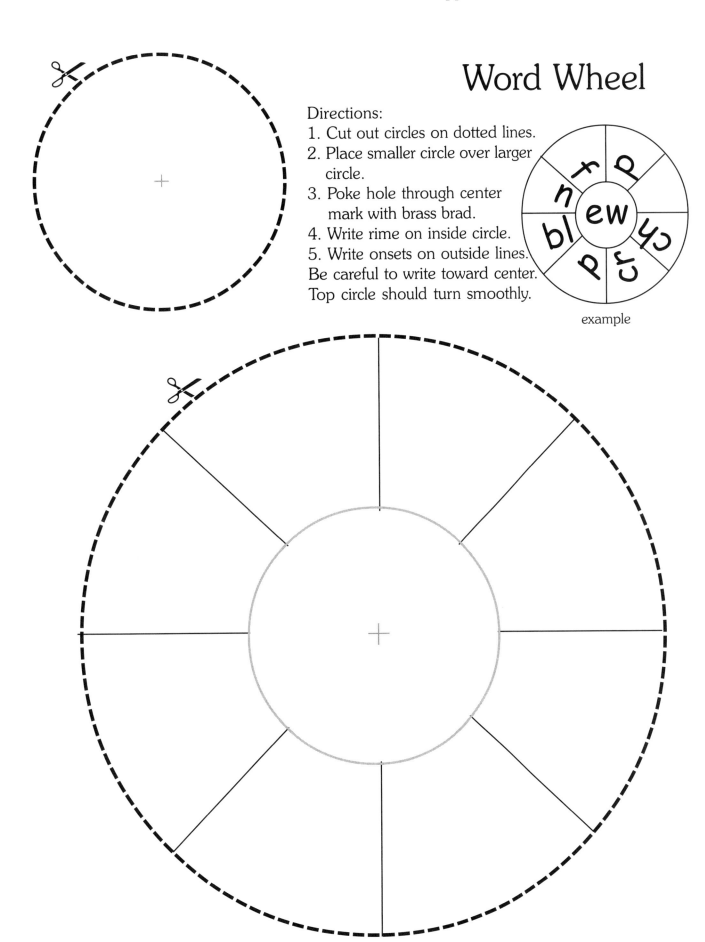

Tic-Tac-Toe

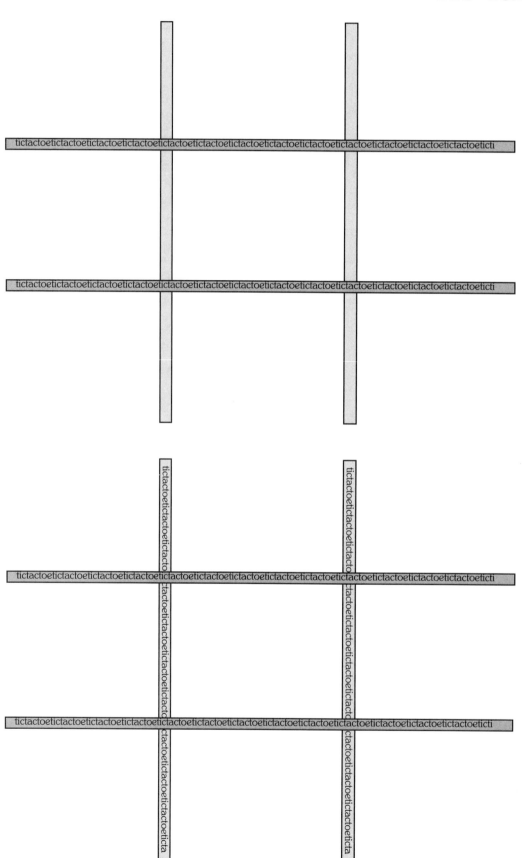

Favorite Phonics Books and Websites

Books

I Knew Two Who Said Moo; A Counting and Rhyming Book by Judi Barrett (2000, Scholastic)

Making Big Words: Multilevel, Hands-On Spelling and Phonics Activities by Patricia M. Cunningham and Dorothy P. Hall (1994, Good Apple)

I love this book, and I used it in my classroom. It has fun, simple lessons and games for teaching phonics to older (3rd- 6th grade) students. Most phonics books and programs ignore older students completely, which makes this even more of a gem.

Websites

http: //www.beginningreading.com

This website is for a reading program for younger children (K-1). You will find really, really good free worksheets for both phonics and sight words.

http: //www.starfall.com

This website is for beginning readers (PreK-2). It is a great place to go if you find that your child needs basic phonics review (simple sounds and blends). The songs, rhymes and graphics are adorable, but definitely for the younger crowd.

FAVORITE BOOKS AND WEBSITES FOR FLUENCY PRACTICE

Here are a few books and websites to get you started choosing books to read with your child. Don't forget to use the ideas discussed in **Chapter 12 How to Teach Fluency Lessons**!

Use a book or a website as a starting point for you and your child. "This book about a girl and her horse sounds interesting…" Then, you and your child can go the library or bookstore together to make your final selection. Please remember to use leveled reading lists as a guide only. If you want to be certain that a book is not too hard or too easy for *your* child, you must do a quick paragraph reading check.

In order for a website to be on this list, it had to be easy to navigate, honest, and have little or no advertising. I also prefer reviews from actual children.

Books:

Dodson, Shireen (1998), *100 Books for Girls to Grow On.* New York, NY: Harper Collins.

The cover of this book says it best: "Lively descriptions of the most inspiring books for girls; Terrific discussion questions to spark conversation; Great ides for book-inspired activities, crafts and field trip." A treasure-trove of information.

Websites

http://www.bookhive.org

If you prefer to search for books by theme (humor, seasons, realistic fiction), this site can't be beat. Take the time to look at the parental notes and comments from readers.

http://www.CarolHurst.com

This comprehensive site is mostly for teachers, but don't let that stop you! Search the amazing database of children's books by theme or subject. Featured Books are not only reviewed, but include discussion topics, activities and ideas.

http://www.educationworld.com/SummerReading

Education World and Barnes and Noble have chosen their favorite books (all conveniently available at Barnes and Noble) and leveled them by grade. The brief description of each book sets this website apart from those of other booksellers.

http: //www.kid-lit.com

Don't have any idea where to start? For readers ages 6 to 14, this site is awesome! Tell the handy-dandy book finder what kind of book you're interested in (gender, age, reading level, keywords, genre, even ethnicity!), and, voila! A list of recommended books! So, if your 4th grade son reading at a 3rd grade level loves Asian cooking- this site will help you find the perfect book! As if that weren't enough, the site lists books by awards. You can find all of, say, the past Coretta Scott King or the Newberry books, in one convenient place.

http: //www.kidsreads.com

You will find it all on this site: games, reviews, excerpts, news about upcoming books, author interviews…The trivia quizzes are what makes it one of my favorite sites. These short, simple quizzes are a fun way to check reading comprehension, and because they are scored on the computer- no extra copying for you!

http: //www.NatomasTutoring.com

Not to brag, but my website is fabulous, and I'll tell you why. Not only do we review new books each month for each grade level/ step, we provide excerpts to print out! Yes, you will know for sure if a book is at the correct instructional reading level for your child (90%- 95% words read correctly). This is especially helpful if you like to purchase books online.

http: //www.spaghettibookclub.org

Reviews by kids for kids plus illustrations- who could ask for anything more? When teachers assign book reviews, this is what they dream of getting. If you have a book in mind that you are hoping your child will choose for fluency practice, read the review to him. A recommendation by another child carries a lot of weight.

PART FOUR

LAST THINGS LAST

Afterword

In **Chapter 4 How to Use This Book** I suggested that you read <u>Tutor Your Own Child to Reading Success!</u> from beginning to end *before* starting to tutor your child. Now you know why! This book contains a lot of information, and unless you have studied reading, many of the ideas and concepts are unfamiliar. If you combine all of the new terminology with the fact that many parents have been lead to believe that only professionals are capable of educating our children, you find parents paralyzed by fear and indecision. We don't want to harm our kids, of course, so we drop them off at school and hope for the best. Then, when we see them struggling, we feel guilty for doing nothing. We wonder, *how can we possibly help our children become good readers?* Even with a step-by-step plan to follow, trying new things and learning new skills can feel awkward or downright scary. It is never easy to step out of our comfort zones.

The good news is that your child will benefit for the rest of her life because of the decisions and commitment you have made. By taking charge of your child's reading and overcoming your own fears, you can do wonders! Take a deep breath and get started tutoring your child- you will find it much easier and more rewarding than you could ever imagine. You can do it!

If you have already begun tutoring your child, way to go! Didn't it feel good to find out- one way or another- which sight words your child knows? Didn't you feel a sense of empowerment when you realized that your son mastered a phonics concept because you taught it to him? Isn't it exciting to hear your daughter read a passage fluently- and understand what it says? These are just some of the rewards of tutoring your child to reading success.

You have already done so much for your child. But, there are two more things that you must do.

First of all, go back and retest. Look in your binder and find the first assessments that you gave your son. Give them to him again. Say, "You have been learning so much these last few weeks (or months)! Let's see how many new words (or how much faster) you now read since we began working on your reading!" You need to know exactly which words and concepts your son has learned, which ones he has yet to master, and whether or not his fluency has improved. Knowing this information allows you to continue to tailor your reading instruction to your child's needs and use your time wisely. You can avoid spinning your wheels- teaching lessons that don't need to be taught- or, worse, not teaching lessons that do need to be taught.

Any progress- no matter how small- should be recognized and applauded. If your daughter has learned five new sight words this month, celebrate! Wow, she read the word *explain* in a story! Let her know that she is making progress, and you are proud of her! Your excitement and approval will give your daughter confidence and fuel her efforts as you continue tutoring, which brings me to my second point...

Don't give up on tutoring! You do not intend to stop tutoring; it just happens, somehow. When you and your child first begin tutoring, the novelty- getting prepared, choosing books, going to your special tutoring place- makes tutoring fun. Tutoring is new and special and you both look forward to it. You are thrilled to see your child's reading progress, and she is reading everything- books, signs, the back of the cereal box. But, then life happens, as it always does. You miss a session here, you miss a session there, the next thing you know, weeks have gone by with no tutoring. Get back on track! Look at your notes, see what lessons you need to teach, and get to it. Tell your daughter that you are sorry that you have let things get in the way and you miss reading with her.

When should you stop tutoring? The simple answer is, continue tutoring until your child is reading at or above grade level. However, don't let that magic day mean an end to everything. Read with your child as long as he is willing to do it. Long after your son has learned sight words and you have taught your last phonics lessons, the two of you can share and discuss books, read interesting passages out loud to one another, and debate whether a book is better than the movie. Our relationships with our children are fraught with change and growth. During some periods, a shared love of reading may be the best way to keep the lines of communication open.

I began this book with a confession, and I'd like to end it with one, as well. The truth is, writing <u>Tutor Your Child to Reading Success</u> has not always been fun. Overall, I have enjoyed the processes of researching, writing and compiling, but some days I wanted to throw up my hands and run away with the circus! As anybody who has had to complete a major project knows, there are a million details to attend to and many, many sacrifices to make. But, even when I had to work into the middle of the night, deal with layout issues, make crucial editing decisions, figure out the balance between enough and too much information, one thing kept me going: I thought about of all the children and parents that might be helped by a book such as this.

I truly hope that Tutor Your Child to Reading Success has been helpful for you and your child. In deciding which information to include in this book, I constantly asked myself what tools, skills and knowledge would a parent need to lead their child from struggle to success? Were you able to help your child cross that bridge? Please write or email me and let me know how you have used this book and what ideas, tips and lessons worked especially well for you and your child. If things did not work so well, let me know that, too. I ask that you share your insights and experiences tutoring your child so that others can gain the knowledge and confidence to help their children become excited and masterful readers.

An entire universe of knowledge, entertainment and joy awaits our children when they become enthusiastic readers.

Good Luck and Stay in Touch!

Bibliography & Recommended Reading

Books

Adams, Marilyn (1990). *Beginning to Read: Thinking and Learning about Print, A Summary* by Stahl, Steven et al. Urbana-Champaign, IL: Center for the Study of Reading.

Cunningham, Patricia M. (1995). *Phonics They Use: Words for Reading and Writing.* New York, NY: HarperCollins College Publishers.

Cunningham, Patricia M. and Hall, Dorothy P. (1994). *Making Big Words: Multilevel, Hands-On Spelling and Phonics Activities.* Torrance, CA: Good Apple.

Durica, Karen Morrow (1996). *Literature Links to Phonics: A Balanced Approach.* Englewood, CO: Teacher Ideas Press.

Fox, Barbara J. (1996). *Strategies for Word Identification: Phonics from a New Perspective.* Englewood Cliffs, NJ: Prentice-Hall, Inc.

Swigert, Nancy B. (2003). *The Source for Reading Fluency.* East Moline, IL: LinguiSystems, Inc.

Magazines

Decodable text- *Where to find it* by Jenkins, Vadasy et al, *The Reading Teacher*, October 2003.

Time for Tutoring? by Dara Chadwick, *Better Homes and Gardens*, November 2004.

Internet

Cromwell, Sharon (1977). *Whole Language and Phonics: Can They Work Together? [Electronic Version].* Education World website: http://www.education-world.com

Hook, Pamela and **Jones**, Sandra D. (2002). *The Importance of Automaticity and Fluency for Efficient Reading Comprehension. [Electronic Reprint].* International Dyslexia Association's newsletter, Perspectives. Winter 2002. Resource Room websites: http//www.resourceroom.net/readspell/2002_automaticity

Moats, Louisa Cook (October 2000). *Whole Language Lives On: The Illusion of "Balanced Reading Instruction" [Electronic Version].* Thomas B. Fordham Foundation website: http://www.edexcellence.com

Rasinski, Timothy V. *Assessing Reading Fluency: Product #ES0414.* Pacific Resource for Education and Learning website: http://www.prel.org (viewed 12/04)

Robb, Laura. *The Myth of Learn to Read/ Read to Learn.* Instructor Magazine reprint from Scholastic website: http:// www.scholastic.com (viewed 1/04).

Shefelbine, John (1988). Information about fluency and fluent readers. Framework for Reading Developmental Studies Center.

Common Reading Disabilities. Delaware County Community College's Reading Department website: http://www.dccc.edu (viewed 1/04)

The Critical Importance of Dolch Sight Words. Picture Me Reading website: http://www.picturemereading.com (viewed 1/04)

Fair Test: National Center for Fair and Open Testing website: http://www.FairTest.org

Listening to Children Read Aloud: Oral Fluency [Electronic Version August 1995]. National Center for Education Statistics website: http://www.nces.ed.gov

National Reading Vocabulary List at Reading Key website: http://www.ReadingKey.com (viewed 1/05)

A New Phonics List- *Sounds/ Spellings (for Teaching Reading).* Read English website: http://www.readenglish.com (viewed 1/05)

Ways to Help Children Improve Reading Fluency. Delaware County Community College's Reading Department website: http://www.dccc.edu (viewed 1/04)

Ways to Help Children Learn to Read. Delaware County Community College's Reading Department website: http://www.dccc.edu (viewed 1/04)

GLOSSARY AND DEFINITIONS

Attention Deficit Disorder (ADD) - a disability in which a child may have problems focusing, sitting still, concentrating, dealing with distractions, finishing tasks and assignments, getting along and working with others, understanding abstract ideas and details, following directions, and multitasking.

alphabetic principles - the third stage of learning to read; occurs when a child understands that word are made up letters.

assessment - a fancy word for *test*

automaticity - fast, accurate and effortless word identification (Hook)

balanced instruction - the "perfect" mixture of phonics and whole language instruction

blends - combination of two or more letters read as one sound: sc, sch, sk, sm, sn, sp, str, sw, br,cr, dr, gr, pr, tr, bl, cl, fl, kl, pl, sl, -sk, -sm, -st, -nd, -nk, -nt, -mp

chunking - decoding a long word by breaking it into syllables; reading a sentence by grouping into smaller phrases

consonant - all letters *except* vowels (*a, e, i, o, u*); formed by using the teeth, tongue, or lips to stop air flow

decoding - reading words by recognizing letter patterns and sounds

digraphs - a pair of letters used to make a new sound: ch, sh, th, ng, wh, kn, ph, wr

dipthongs - a pair of vowels pronounced as one sound: ay, ai, au, ea, ee, ie, oa, oi, ou

Discovery Learning - self-generated learning; a child discovers the need for more information to answer a question or solve a problem

Dysgraphia - a learning disability resulting from a disorder in the part of the brain that controls writing; usually affects reading as well

Dyslexia - a learning disability in which people have difficulty distinguishing the sounds that make up words

fluency - reading speed and accuracy

formal tutoring - tutoring that occurs during planned times with a specific, goal-oriented agenda

frustration reading level- level at which one reads less than 90% of the words in a text

independent reading level- level at which one can read 95% or more of the words in a text

informal tutoring - tutoring that occurs outside of planned, or formal, tutoring sessions

instructional reading level- level at which one can read 90-95% of the words in a text

intonation - reading characterized by the rise and fall of pitch

long vowel sounds - vowel sounds that take longer to say; when the vowel "says its name" (*tame, team, bone, line, dude*)

manipulatives - materials (i.e. blocks and tiles) handled by students; used primarily in elementary school math instruction

norm-referenced tests- tests designed so that half the testing population scores above 50% and half scores below 50%

onset - the initial consonant or consonant blend of a word (*tr* is the onset of *train*)

orthographic awareness- the fourth stage of learning to read; occurs when a child realizes that writing has meaning and structure

phonemes- the smallest bits of sounds; usually represented by letters.

phonemic awareness- the second stage of learning to read; occurs when a child understands that sounds have symbols (letters) that represent them.

phonics- The direct instruction of letters and their sounds to teach reading

phonological awareness- the first stage of learning to read; occurs when a child becomes aware of sounds

prompting- helping a child or student by telling them the word or answer

proper noun- names a specific person, place or thing (*White House* is a proper noun; *house* is a common noun)

prosody- reading with meaning, animation and expression; includes changes in pitch, stressing certain words, pausing at commas, stopping at periods, raising one's voice when asking a question

r-controlled vowels- vowel sounds change when followed by an *r*: ar, air, are, ear, eer, er, ir, ire, or, oor, ore, our, ur

rime- the vowel and final consonants of a word; (*ain* is the rime of *train*)

rubric- a guide used to score subjective assignments, projects, tests

short vowel sounds- vowel sounds that are said quickly; occur when the sound of the vowel is expressed (*mat, red, in, mop, cut*)

sight words- the most commonly spoken and written words in the English language; comprise an enormous amount of children's reading, and should be memorized and read *on sight*

sneaky teaching- teaching planned without children's knowledge; often occurs without children realizing that they are learning

soft and hard consonant sounds (*c and g*)
> - soft: *c* sounds like s *(cellar)*, soft *g* sounds like j *(gem)*
> - *interesting* rule: *c* and *g* are soft when followed by *e, i, y (ceiling, gelatin, city, giant, cylinder, gypsy)*
> - hard: *c* sounds like *k (cat)*, *g* sounds like g *(got)*
> - *interesting* rule: *c* and *g* are hard when followed by a, o, u *(cake, game, corn, gory, cut, gut)*

syllable
> - a sound that can be said without interruption; children should be taught to decode big words by breaking them into syllables (*confusion* is *con/fu/sion*)
> - *bat* (1 syllable), *batter* (2 syllables), *battery* (3 syllables)

teachable moment- an unexpected opportunity for teaching and learning

tracking- physically keeping one's place while reading

vowel- a, e, i, o, u, sometimes y; made by allowing free airflow through the mouth

wait time- allowing a few moments to pass before giving a student an answer or calling on a student to answer a question

Whole Language- teaching reading by using whole texts; this method does not teach direct instruction of phonics, punctuation, spelling or grammar

word family- a group of words that share the same rime (maid, raid, laid, staid)

Index

Postal orders: Natomas Tutoring, Dept. B
2121 Natomas Crossing Drive
Suite 200-159
Sacramento, CA 95834
(916) 806-9663
(Please send this form)

FOR ALL OTHER ORDERING OPTIONS,
PLEASE VISIT OUR WEBSITE www.NatomasTutoring.com

Tutor Your Child to Reading Success $29.95 ea. book
                                           Buy 4 copies, 1 free!   _____

Assessments (Tutor and Student) $9.95 ea.
         ☒ Sight Words
         ☒ Phonics   _____
         ☒ Fluency   _____
                                                                       _____

The Homework Workbook $12.95 ea. workbook   _____
(from Take Back the Night!
Slaying the Homework Dragon seminar)

Calling All Parents!
10 Things Your Child's Teacher $9.95 ea. handbook
Really, Really Wants to Tell You!   Buy 4 copies, 1 free!   _____

Sales Tax: Please add 7.75%
                 for orders shipped to California addresses   _____

Shipping: $4 for 1ˢᵗ book; $2 each additional book
                 $3 for 1ˢᵗ assessment, workbook or handbook;
                 $1 each additional
                 (Please call for International shipping rates)   _____

                                           TOTAL   [   ]

Payment: ☒ **Visa**   ☒ **MasterCard**
                ☒ **Check** (payable to Natomas Tutoring)   ☒ **Money Order**

        Number:_____-_____-_____-_____

        Name on Card:_____Exp. Date: _____

Ship to: Name:_____
Address:_____
_____
City:_____   State_____   Zip_____